PHILIP'S

FAMILY WORLD ATLAS

First published in Great Britain in 1994
by George Philip Limited,
an imprint of Reed Consumer Books Limited,
Michelin House, 81 Fulham Road, London SW3 6RB
and Auckland, Melbourne, Singapore and Toronto

Cartography by Philip's

Copyright © 1994 Reed International Books Limited

ISBN 0 540 05825 4

A CIP catalogue record for this book is available from
the British Library

Printed in China

CONTENTS

iv   **World Statistics: Countries**

I   **Key to Map Symbols**
     The World: Physical

2–3   **The World: Political** 1:80M

4   **The Arctic and**
     Antarctica 1:50M

5   **Europe: Political** 1:20M

6–7   **Scandinavia and the Baltic**
     Lands 1:5M

8–9   **England and Wales** 1:2M

10   **Scotland** 1:2M

11   **Ireland** 1:2M

12   **France** 1:5M

13   **Spain and Portugal** 1:5M

14–15   **Italy and the Balkan**
     States 1:5M

16–17   **Central Europe** 1:5M

18–19   **Eastern Europe, Russia and**
     Central Asia 1:20M

20   **Asia: Political** 1:50M

21   **Japan** 1:10M
     Southern Japan 1:5M

22   **China** 1:20M

23   **South-east Asia** 1:20M

24   **Southern Asia** 1:20M

25   **South-west Asia** 1:20M

26–27   **Northern Africa** 1:15M

28–29   **Central and Southern**
     Africa 1:15M

30   **Africa: Political** 1:40M

31   **New Zealand** 1:6M
     New Zealand and
     S.W. Pacific 1:60M
     Fiji, Tonga and Samoan
     Islands 1:12M

32–33   **Australia** 1:12M

34–35   **Canada** 1:15M
     Alaska 1:30M

36–37   **United States** 1:12M
     Hawaii 1:10M

38–39   **Mexico, Central America**
     and the West Indies 1:15M
     Leeward Islands,
     Windward Islands,
     Trinidad and Tobago,
     and Jamaica 1:5M
     Panama Canal 1:1M

40–41   **South America – North** 1:16M

42   **South America – South** 1:16M

43–48   **Index**

WORLD STATISTICS: COUNTRIES

This alphabetical list includes all the countries and territories of the world. If a territory is not completely independent, then the country it is associated with is named. The area figures give the total area of land, inland water and ice. Units for areas and populations are thousands. The figures are the latest available, usually 1991.

Country/Territory	Area km² Thousands	Population Thousands	Capital
Afghanistan	648	16,450	Kabul
Albania	28.8	3,335	Tirana
Algeria	2,382	25,680	Algiers
American Samoa (US)	0.2	43	Pago Pago
Andorra	0.45	58	Andorra la Vella
Angola	1,247	8,668	Luanda
Anguilla (UK)	0.2	9	The Valley
Antigua & Barbuda	0.44	64	St John's
Argentina	2,767	32,713	Buenos Aires
Armenia	29.8	3,305	Yerevan
Aruba (Neths.)	0.19	64	Oranjestad
Australia	7,687	17,292	Canberra
Austria	83.9	7,796	Vienna
Azerbaijan	86.6	7,100	Baku
Azores (Port)	2.2	260	Ponta Delgada
Bahamas	13.9	259	Nassau
Bahrain	0.68	516	Manama
Bangladesh	144	122,000	Dacca
Barbados	0.43	258	Bridgetown
Belau (US)	0.46	15	Koror
Belgium	30.5	10,004	Brussels
Belize	23	194	Belmopan
Belorussia	207.6	10,374	Minsk
Benin	113	4,886	Porto-Novo
Bermuda (UK)	0.05	58	Hamilton
Bhutan	47	1,464	Thimphu
Bolivia	1,099	7,340	La Paz/Sucre
Bosnia-Herzegovina	51.2	4,366	Sarajevo
Botswana	582	1,348	Gaborone
Brazil	8,512	153,322	Brasilia
Brunei	5.8	398	Bandar Seri Begawan
Bulgaria	111	8,975	Sofia
Burkina Faso	274	9,242	Ouagadougou
Burma (Myanmar)	679	42,112	Rangoon
Burundi	27.8	5,653	Bujumbura
Cambodia	181	7,146	Phnom Penh
Cameroon	475	11,881	Yaoundé
Canada	9,976	27,300	Ottawa
Canary Is. (Spain)	7.3	1,700	Las Palmas/Santa Cruz
Cape Verde Is.	4	380	Praia
Cayman Is. (UK)	0.26	27	Georgetown
Central African Rep.	623	3,086	Bangui
Chad	1,284	5,826	Ndjamena
Chile	757	13,386	Santiago
China	9,597	1,151,487	Beijing (Peking)
Colombia	1,139	32,841	Bogotá
Comoros	2.2	570	Moroni
Congo	342	2,350	Brazzaville
Cook Is. (NZ)	0.24	18	Avarua
Costa Rica	51.1	3,064	San José
Croatia	56.5	4,784	Zagreb
Cuba	111	10,732	Havana
Cyprus	9.3	710	Nicosia
Czech Republic	78.9	10,310	Prague
Denmark	43.1	5,154	Copenhagen
Djibouti	23.2	346	Djibouti
Dominica	0.75	72	Roseau
Dominican Republic	48.7	7,197	Santo Domingo
Ecuador	284	10,782	Quito
Egypt	1,001	54,688	Cairo
El Salvador	21	5,278	San Salvador
Equatorial Guinea	28.1	356	Malabo
Eritrea	94	3,500	Asmera
Estonia	44.7	1,595	Tallinn
Ethiopia	1,128	49,290	Addis Ababa
Falkland Is. (UK)	12.2	2	Stanley
Faroe Is. (Den.)	1.4	48	Tórshavn
Fiji	18.3	741	Suva
Finland	338	5,029	Helsinki
France	552	57,049	Paris
French Guiana (Fr.)	90	102	Cayenne
French Polynesia (Fr.)	4	206	Papeete
Gabon	268	1,168	Libreville
Gambia, The	11.3	902	Banjul
Georgia	69.7	5,571	Tbilisi
Germany	357	80,275	Berlin
Ghana	239	15,336	Accra
Gibraltar (UK)	0.007	30	-
Greece	132	10,330	Athens
Greenland (Den.)	2,176	60	Godthåb
Grenada	0.34	91	St George's
Guadeloupe (Fr.)	1.7	345	Basse-Terre
Guam (US)	0.54	145	Agana
Guatemala	109	9,467	Guatemala City
Guinea	246	5,880	Conakry
Guinea-Bissau	36.1	1,001	Bissau
Guyana	215	802	Georgetown
Haiti	27.8	6,625	Port-au-Prince
Honduras	112	5,264	Tegucigalpa
Hong Kong (UK)	1.1	5,755	-
Hungary	93	10,344	Budapest
Iceland	103	258	Reykjavik
India	3,288	866,352	Delhi
Indonesia	1,905	193,560	Jakarta
Iran	1,648	57,727	Tehran
Iraq	438	19,525	Baghdad
Ireland	70.3	3,522	Dublin
Israel	27	4,946	Jerusalem
Italy	301	57,764	Rome
Ivory Coast	322	12,360	Abidjan
Jamaica	11	2,376	Kingston
Japan	378	124,017	Tokyo
Jordan	89.2	3,664	Amman
Kazakhstan	2,717	17,104	Alma Ata
Kenya	580	25,006	Nairobi
Kirghizia	198.5	4,568	Bishkek
Kiribati	0.72	71	Tarawa
Korea, North	121	21,815	Pyongyang
Korea, South	99	43,286	Seoul
Kuwait	17.8	2,204	Kuwait City
Laos	237	4,261	Vientiane
Latvia	65	2,685	Riga
Lebanon	10.4	3,385	Beirut
Lesotho	30.4	1,813	Maseru
Liberia	111	2,639	Monrovia
Libya	1,760	4,706	Tripoli
Liechtenstein	0.16	29	Vaduz
Lithuania	65.2	3,789	Vilnius
Luxembourg	2.6	385	Luxembourg
Macau (Port.)	0.02	446	-
Macedonia	25.3	2,174	Skopje
Madagascar	587	12,032	Antananarivo
Madeira (Port.)	0.81	280	Funchal
Malawi	118	8,556	Lilongwe
Malaysia	330	18,178	Kuala Lumpur
Maldives	0.3	226	Malé
Mali	1,240	8,707	Bamako
Malta	0.32	356	Valletta
Mariana Is. (US)	0.48	22	Saipan
Marshall Is. (US)	0.18	48	Dalap-Uliga-Darrit
Martinique (Fr.)	1.1	345	Fort-de-France
Mauritania	1,025	2,025	Nouakchott
Mauritius	1.9	1,087	Port Louis
Mayotte (Fr.)	0.37	84	Mamoundzou
Mexico	1,958	83,306	Mexico City
Micronesia, Fed. St.	0.7	107	Palikir
Moldavia	33.7	4,458	Kishinev
Monaco	0.002	30	Monaco
Mongolia	1,567	2,250	Ulan Bator
Montserrat (UK)	0.1	13	Plymouth
Morocco	447	25,668	Rabat
Mozambique	802	16,128	Maputo
Namibia	824	1,781	Windhoek
Nauru	0.02	10	Yaren
Nepal	141	19,401	Katmandu
Netherlands	41.5	15,239	Amsterdam
Neths. Antilles (Neths.)	0.99	191	Willemstad
New Caledonia (Fr.)	19	172	Nouméa
New Zealand	269	3,406	Wellington
Nicaragua	130	3,999	Managua
Niger	1,267	7,911	Niamey
Nigeria	924	88,515	Lagos/Abuja
Norway	324	4,262	Oslo
Oman	212	1,583	Muscat
Pakistan	796	115,844	Islamabad
Panama	77.1	2,466	Panama City
Papua New Guinea	463	3,964	Port Moresby
Paraguay	407	4,397	Asunción
Peru	1,285	21,945	Lima
Philippines	300	62,868	Manila
Poland	313	38,245	Warsaw
Portugal	92.4	10,387	Lisbon
Puerto Rico (US)	9	3,366	San Juan
Qatar	11	368	Doha
Réunion (Fr.)	2.5	607	St-Denis
Romania	238	22,974	Bucharest
Russia	17,075	149,527	Moscow
Rwanda	26.3	7,125	Kigali
St Christopher/Nevis	0.3	42	Basseterre
St Lucia	0.62	153	Castries
St Pierre & Miquelon (Fr.)	0.24	6	St Pierre
St Vincent/Grenadines	0.39	114	Kingstown
San Marino	0.06	24	San Marino
São Tomé & Príncipe	0.96	124	São Tomé
Saudi Arabia	2,150	15,381	Riyadh
Senegal	197	7,625	Dakar
Seychelles	0.46	67	Victoria
Sierra Leone	71.7	4,243	Freetown
Singapore	0.62	3,003	Singapore
Slovak Republic	49	5,297	Bratislava
Slovenia	20.3	1,975	Ljubljana
Solomon Is.	28.9	325	Honiara
Somalia	638	8,051	Mogadishu
South Africa	1,221	38,858	Pretoria
Spain	505	39,025	Madrid
Sri Lanka	65.6	17,190	Colombo
Sudan	2,506	25,204	Khartoum
Surinam	163	403	Paramaribo
Swaziland	17.4	828	Mbabane
Sweden	450	8,635	Stockholm
Switzerland	41.3	6,791	Bern
Syria	185	12,529	Damascus
Taiwan	36	20,659	Taipei
Tajikistan	143.1	5,680	Dushanbe
Tanzania	945	25,635	Dar es Salaam
Thailand	513	57,151	Bangkok
Togo	56.8	3,773	Lomé
Tonga	0.75	103	Nuku'alofa
Trinidad & Tobago	5.1	1,253	Port of Spain
Tunisia	164	8,237	Tunis
Turkey	779	60,777	Ankara
Turkmenistan	488.1	3,838	Ashkhabad
Turks & Caicos Is. (UK)	0.43	12	Grand Turk
Tuvalu	0.03	10	Funafuti
Uganda	236	18,795	Kampala
Ukraine	603.7	51,940	Kiev
United Arab Emirates	83.6	1,629	Abu Dhabi
United Kingdom	243.3	57,564	London
United States	9,373	249,928	Washington
Uruguay	177	3,112	Montevideo
Uzbekistan	447.4	21,627	Tashkent
Vanuatu	12.2	154	Port Vila
Venezuela	912	19,787	Caracas
Vietnam	332	66,200	Hanoi
Virgin Is. (UK)	0.15	17	Road Town
Virgin Is. (US)	0.34	117	Charlotte Amalie
Wallis & Futuna Is. (Fr.)	0.2	18	Mata-Utu
Western Sahara (Mor.)	266	197	El Aiun
Western Samoa	2.8	161	Apia
Yemen	528	12,544	Sana
Yugoslavia	102.3	10,642	Belgrade
Zaïre	2,345	38,631	Kinshasa
Zambia	753	8,319	Lusaka
Zimbabwe	391	10,079	Harare

GENERAL REFERENCE

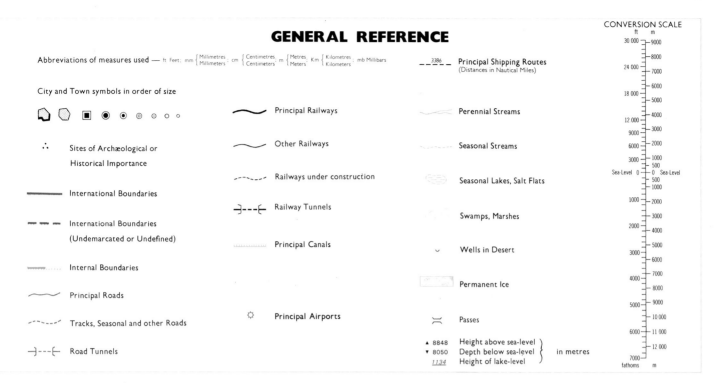

Abbreviations of measures used — ft Feet; mm {Millimetres / Millimeters} cm {Centimetres / Centimeters} m {Metres / Meters} Km {Kilometres / Kilometers} mb Millibars

City and Town symbols in order of size

Sites of Archæological or Historical Importance

International Boundaries

International Boundaries (Undemarcated or Undefined)

Internal Boundaries

Principal Roads

Tracks, Seasonal and other Roads

Road Tunnels

Principal Railways

Other Railways

Railways under construction

Railway Tunnels

Principal Canals

Principal Airports

Principal Shipping Routes (Distances in Nautical Miles)

Perennial Streams

Seasonal Streams

Seasonal Lakes, Salt Flats

Swamps, Marshes

Wells in Desert

Permanent Ice

Passes

▲ 8848 Height above sea-level
▼ 8050 Depth below sea-level } in metres
1134 Height of lake-level

CONVERSION SCALE

THE WORLD
Physical
1:150 000 000

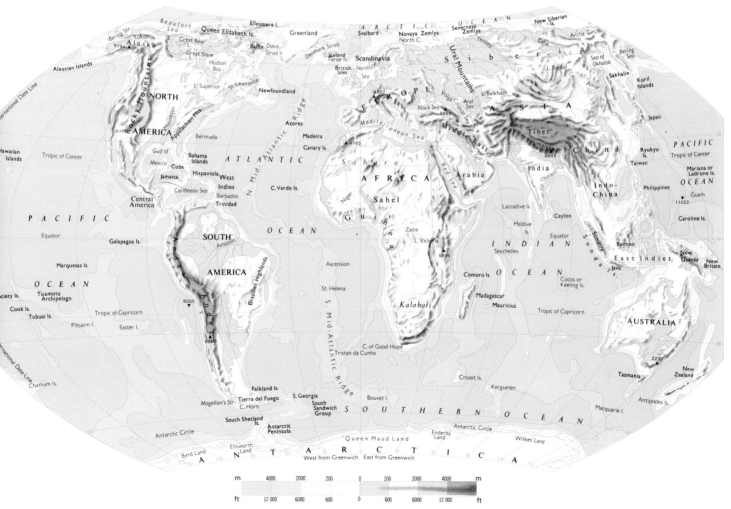

Projection: Hammer Equal Area

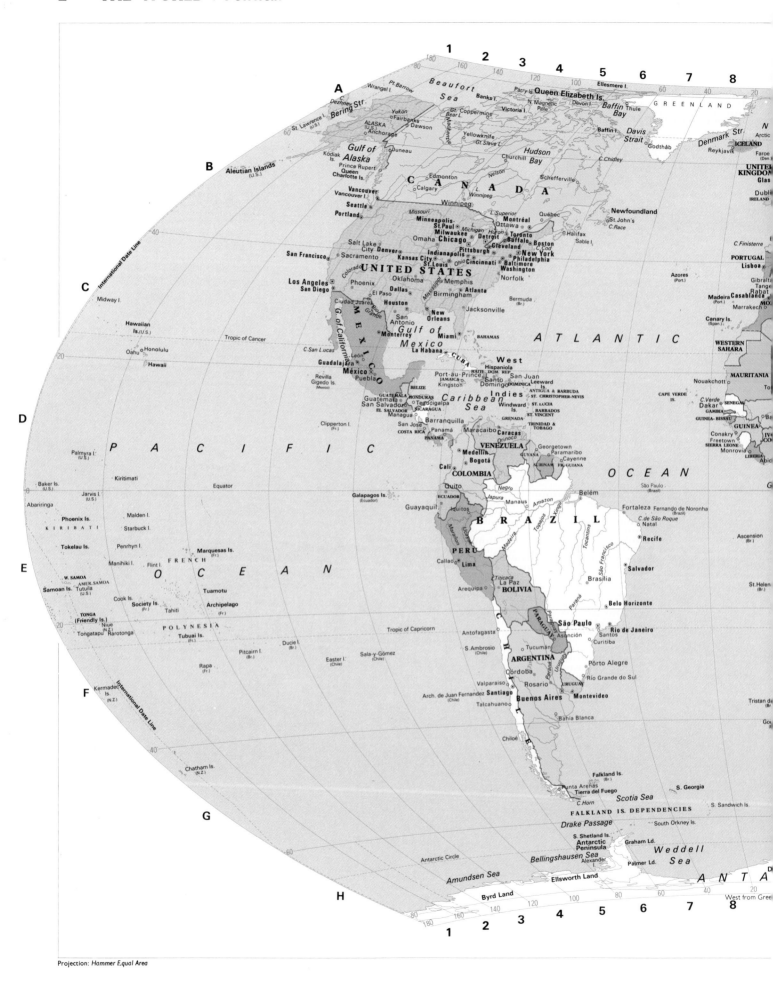

Projection: *Hammer Equal Area*

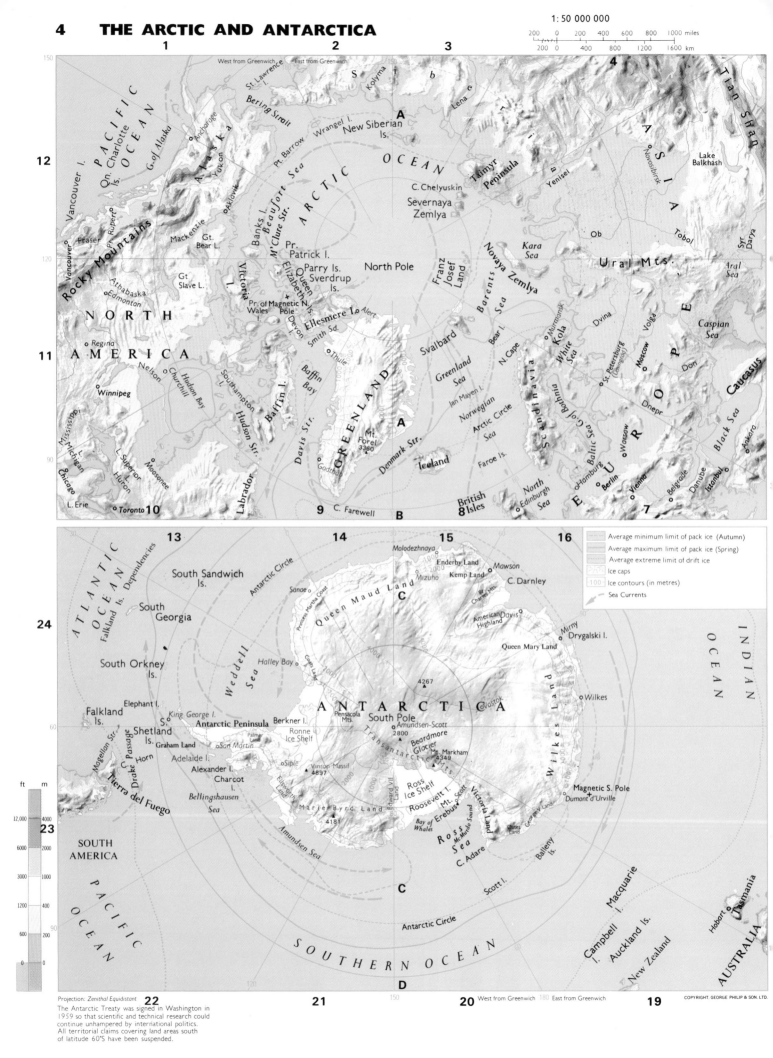

1 : 50 000 000

Projection: *Zenithal Equidistant* **22**

The Antarctic Treaty was signed in Washington in
1959 so that scientific and technical research could
continue unhampered by international politics.
All territorial claims covering land areas south
of latitude 60°S have been suspended.

COPYRIGHT. GEORGE PHILIP & SON. LTD.

	Average minimum limit of pack ice (Autumn)
	Average maximum limit of pack ice (Spring)
	Average extreme limit of drift ice
	Ice caps
100	Ice contours (in metres)
	Sea Currents

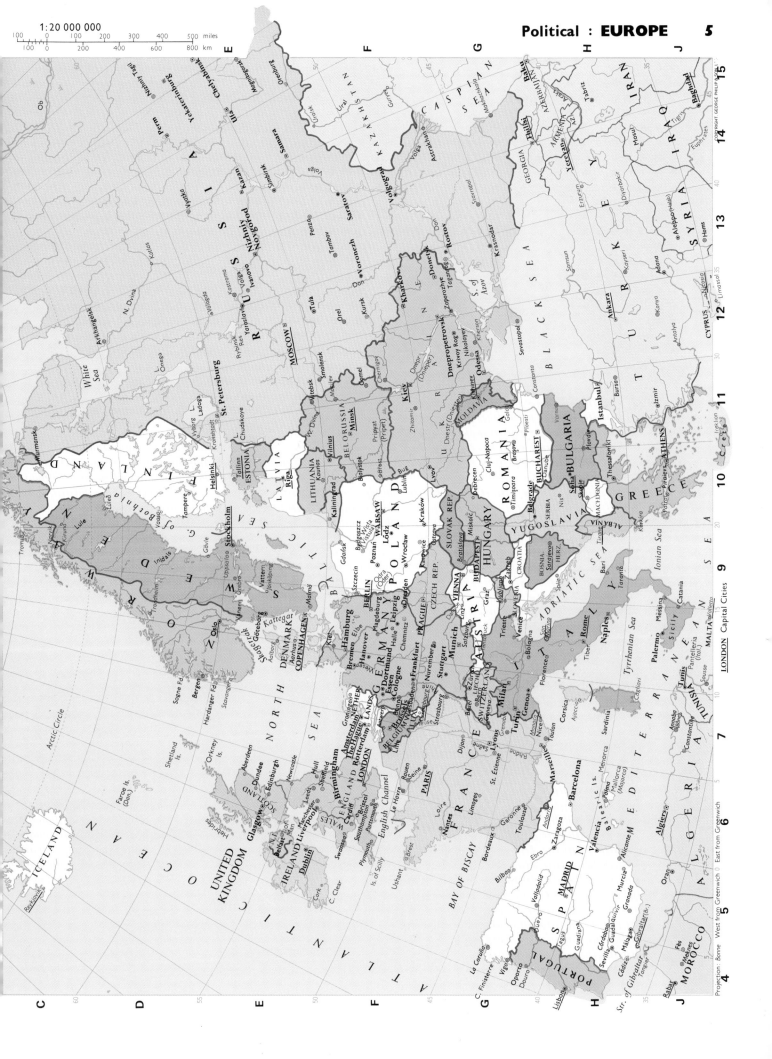

NORWEGIAN SEA

FINLAND · LAPLAND · SWEDEN · NORWAY · SVERIGE

KESKI-SUOMEN · KUOPIO · VAASA · VINHLI · POHJOIS

Oulu · Kemi · Tornio · Haparanda · Luleå · Boden · Piteå · Skellefteå · Umeå · Örnsköldsvik · Härnösand

Rovaniemi · Kemijärvi · Kajaani · Iisalmi · Kuopio

Nordkapp · Hammerfest · Vadsø · Vardø · Tromsø · Narvik · Bodø · Mo · Mosjøen · Namsos · Steinkjer · Levanger · Trondheim · Kristiansund · Molde · Ålesund

Kiruna · Gällivare · Malmberget · Storuman · Lycksele · Östersund · Storsjön · Flåsjön

NORRBOTTEN · VÄSTERBOTTEN · JÄMTLAND · MEDELPAD · ÅNGERMANLAND · HÄLSINGLAND · N-TRØNDELAG · S-TRØNDELAG

Lapphavet · Kvænangen · Fugløysund · Lofoten · Vesterålen · Vestfjorden · Moskenstraumen · Røst · Værøy

Tanafjorden · Laksefjorden · Porsangen · FINNMARK

Lakselv · Karasjok · Kautokeino · Enontekiö · Kittilä · Sodankylä · Kemijärvi · Kittilä

Torneträsk · Storra Lulevatten · Uddjaur · Storavan · Arvidsjaur · Älvsbyn

Arctic Circle

Laki · Hekla · 1491 Torfa-jökull · Vatnajökull · Hofsjökull · Langjökull · Eiríksjökull 1675 · Myrdalsjökull · Surtsey

ICELAND on the same scale as general map

Ísafjarðardjúp · Arnarfjörður · Breiðafjörður · Faxaflói · Reykjanes · Keflavík · Reykjavík · Akranes · Hafnarfjörður · Borgarnes · Akureyri · Sauðárkrókur · Siglufjörður · Húsavík · Seyðisfjörður · Egilsstaðir · Höfn · Vestmannaeyjar

Húnaflói · Skagafjörður · Eyjafjörður · Axarfjörður · Héraðsflói · Skjálfandi

West from 18 Greenwich

NORTH SEA

IRISH SEA

North Channel

SCOTLAND

ENGLAND

WALES

Southern Uplands

Cheviot Hills

NORTHUMBERLAND

CUMBRIA

Cumbrian Mts.

Pennines

NORTH YORKSHIRE

N. York Moors

DURHAM

TYNE & WEAR

CLEVELAND (Teesside)

HUMBERSIDE

Holderness

LINCOLN

LINCOLN Wolds

NOTTS

DERBY

SOUTH YORKSHIRE

W. YORKSHIRE

GREATER MANCHESTER

LANCASHIRE

MERSEYSIDE

CHESHIRE

STAFFORD

CLWYD

GWYNEDD

Anglesey

Isle of Man

Ochil Hills
Lammermuir Hills
Moorfoot Hills
Pentland Hills

Galloway

Inveraray
Lochgilphead
Gigha I.
Jura
Sound of Jura
Crinan
Tarbert
Islay
Campbeltown
Mull of Kintyre
Kintyre
Arran
Goat Fell 874
Ailsa Craig
B. Lomond
L. Lomond
Helensburgh
Dumbarton
Clydebank
Greenock
Gourock
Port Glasgow
Paisley
Glasgow
Rutherglen
Hamilton
Motherwell
Wishaw
Airdrie
Coatbridge
Stirling
Falkirk
Kirkcaldy
Kinross
Dunfermline
Leith
Edinburgh
Musselburgh
Haddington
Dunbar
North Berwick
Bass Rock
Fife Ness
Anstruther
L. Leven
Alloa
Forth
L. Katrine
Trossachs

Peebles
Galashiels
Selkirk
Hawick
Jedburgh
Kelso
Coldstream
Lauder
Lanark
Carstairs
Leadhills
Sanquhar
Nith
Dumfries
Annan
Dalbeattie
Castle Douglas
Kirkcudbright
Newton Stewart
Wigtown
Whithorn
Stranraer
Portpatrick
Merrick 843
Cree
Doon
Ayr
Irvine
Kilmarnock
Saltcoats
Largs

Berwick-upon-Tweed
Holy I.
Farne Is.
Bamburgh
Alnwick
Coquet
Morpeth
Ashington
Blyth
Tyne
Newcastle
Wallsend
Tynemouth
South Shields
Gateshead
Sunderland
Houghton-le-Spring
Blaydon
Hexham
Consett
Durham
Peterlee
Hartlepool
Billingham
Stockton
Middlesbrough
Redcar
Whitby
Darlington
Bishop Auckland
Barnard Castle
Richmond
Northallerton
Thirsk
Scarborough
Filey
Bridlington
Flamborough Hd.
Pickering
Malton
Helmsley
York
Ripon
Harrogate
Knaresborough
Pontefract
Selby
Goole
Scunthorpe
Doncaster
Rotherham
Sheffield
Chesterfield
Leeds
Bradford
Halifax
Huddersfield
Dewsbury
Wakefield
Barnsley
Keighley
Skipton
Settle
Ingleborough 723
Pen-y-Ghent 693
Whernside 704

Carlisle
Penrith
Keswick
Skiddaw 931
Helvellyn 950
Sca Fell 978
Workington
Maryport
Whitehaven
St. Bee's Hd.
Seascale
Millom
Barrow
Walney I.
Ulverston
Windermere
Ambleside
Kendal
Morecambe
Lancaster
Fleetwood
Cleveleys
Blackpool
Lytham-St. Annes
Preston
Southport
Formby Pt.
Bootle
Wallasey
Birkenhead
Liverpool
St. Helens
Widnes
Warrington
Wigan
Bolton
Bury
Rochdale
Oldham
Manchester
Salford
Stockport
Stalybridge
Glossop
Buxton
Macclesfield
Crewe
Nantwich
Northwich
Chester
Ellesmere Port
Wrexham
Mold
Flint
Rhyl
Colwyn Bay
Llandudno
Conwy
Bangor
Beaumaris
Amlwch
Holyhead
Holy I.
Caernarfon
Menai Strait
Snowdon 1085
Ffestiniog
Blaenau Ffestiniog
Bala
Harlech
Pwllheli
Nefyn
Porthmadog

Scunthorpe
Grimsby
Immingham
Cleethorpes
Spurn Hd.
Withernsea
Hornsea
Hull
Beverley
Driffield
Market Rasen
Gainsborough
Retford
Worksop
Mansfield
Sutton-in-Ashfield
Alfreton
Ilkeston
Heanor
Belper
Derby
Nottingham
Newark
Lincoln
Sleaford
Grantham
Boston
Stoke-on-Trent
Newcastle-under-Lyme
Leek
Uttoxeter
Stafford
Whitchurch
Oswestry

The Wash
Cromer
North Walsham
Sheringham
Hunstanton Wells
Sandringham
Skegness
Mablethorpe
Alford
Louth
Horncastle
Woodhall

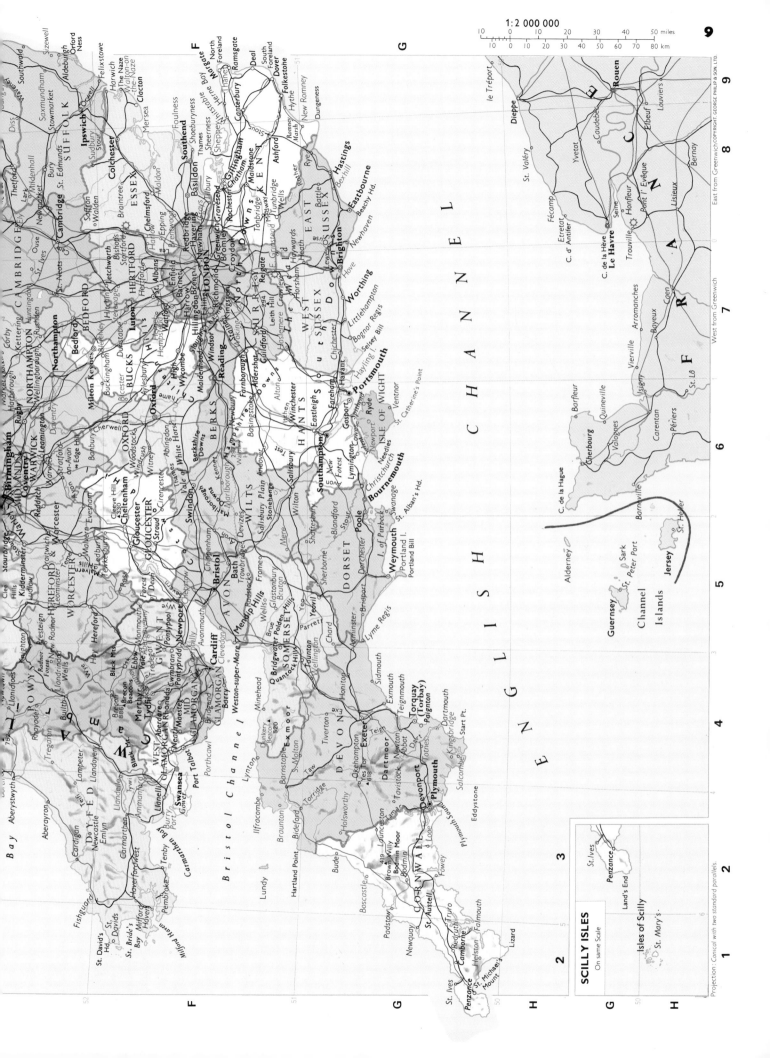

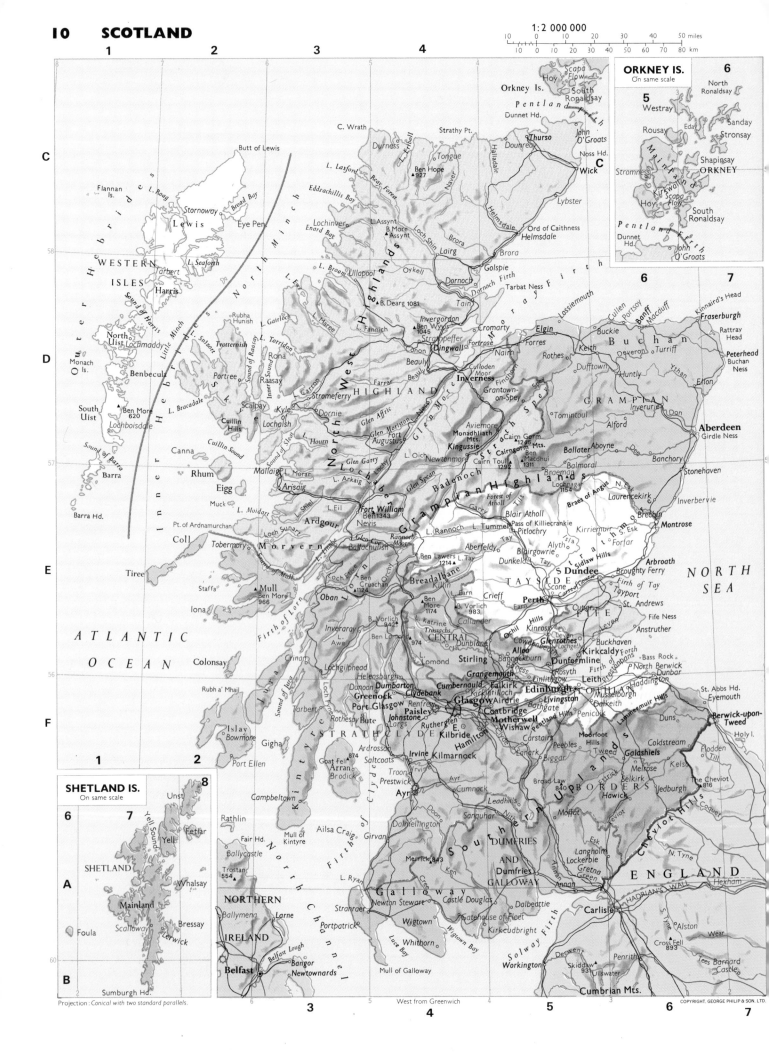

1 : 2 000 000

ORKNEY IS.
On same scale

SHETLAND IS.
On same scale

Projection : Conical with two standard parallels.

West from Greenwich

1 : 2 000 000

Projection : Conical with two standard parallels.

West from Greenwich

COPYRIGHT. GEORGE PHILIP & SON, LTD.

Towns underlined in Northern Ireland give their
names to the Districts in which they stand
The remaining Districts are :—

1 Fermanagh	5 Castlereagh
2 Moyle	6 Ards
3 Newtownabbey	7 Down
4 North Down	8 Newry & Mourne

1:5 000 000

Miles scale: 20 10 0 20 40 60 80 100 miles
Kilometres scale: 40 20 0 40 80 120 160 km

FRENCH DEPARTMENTS

Ai.	01	Ain
Ai.	02	Aisne
Al.	03	Allier
A.H.P.	04	Alpes-de-Haute-Provence
H.A.	05	Hautes-Alpes
A.M.	06	Alpes-Maritimes
Ard.	07	Ardèche
Ard.	08	Ardennes
A.	09	Ariège
Aud.	10	Aube
	11	Aude
	12	Aveyron
B.Rh.	13	Bouches-du-Rhône
Cal.	14	Calvados
	15	Cantal
Ch.	16	Charente
Ch.M.	17	Charente-Maritime
Che.	18	Cher
	19	Corrèze
	20	Corse a) Haute-Corse b) Corse du Sud
C.O.	21	Côte-d'Or
C.A.	22	Côtes d'Armor
	23	Creuse
Do.	24	Dordogne
Dr.	25	Doubs
	26	Drôme
E.L.	27	Eure
	28	Eure-et-Loir
Fi.	29	Finistère
Ge.	30	Gard
Gi.	31	Haute-Garonne
	32	Gers
	33	Gironde
H.V.	34	Hérault
I.V.	35	Ille-et-Vilaine
	36	Indre
I.L.	37	Indre-et-Loire
	38	Isère
	39	Jura
	40	Landes
L.C.	41	Loir-et-Cher
Lo.	42	Loire
H.L.	43	Haute-Loire
L.A.	44	Loire-Atlantique
Loi.	45	Loiret
	46	Lot
L.G.	47	Lot-et-Garonne
Loz.	48	Lozère
M.L.	49	Maine-et-Loire
	50	Manche
Ma.	51	Marne
H.Ma.	52	Haute-Marne
May.	53	Mayenne
M.M.	54	Meurthe-et-Moselle
Me.	55	Meuse
	56	Morbihan
Mos.	57	Moselle
Ni.	58	Nièvre
No.	59	Nord
O.	60	Oise
	61	Orne
P.C.	62	Pas-de-Calais
P.D.	63	Puy-de-Dôme
P.A.	64	Pyrénées-Atlantiques
H.P.	65	Hautes-Pyrénées
P.O.	66	Pyrénées-Orientales
B.R.	67	Bas-Rhin
H.R.	68	Haut-Rhin
Rh.	69	Rhône
H.S.	70	Haute-Saône
S.L.	71	Saône-et-Loire
	72	Sarthe
	73	Savoie
H.Sa.	74	Haute-Savoie
	75	Paris
S.Me.	76	Seine-Maritime
S.M.	77	Seine-et-Marne
	78	Yvelines
D.S.	79	Deux-Sèvres
So.	80	Somme
T.	81	Tarn
T.G.	82	Tarn-et-Garonne
	83	Var
Va.	84	Vaucluse
Ve.	85	Vendée
Vi.	86	Vienne
H.V.	87	Haute-Vienne
	88	Vosges
Y.	89	Yonne
B.	90	Belfort
Es.	91	Essonne
	92	Hauts-de-Seine
S.St-D.	93	Seine-St-Denis
V.M.	94	Val-de-Marne
V.O.	95	Val-d'Oise

CORSICA
On same scale

Corse — Haute-Corse — Corse du Sud
Bastia, Calvi, Corte, Mte. Rotondo 2625, Mt. Cinto 2710, Ajaccio, Bonifacio, Porto Vecchio

East from Greenwich

Major labels on map:

GERMANY, BELGIUM, SWITZERLAND, SPAIN, ITALY, LIGURIA

ENGLISH CHANNEL, BAY OF BISCAY, MEDITERRANEAN SEA, Golfe du Lion, Golfe de Gascogne

Regions: PICARDIE, NORMANDIE, BRETAGNE, ORLÉANAIS, TOURAINE, POITOU, AUNIS, SAINTONGE, ANGOUMOIS, GUYENNE, GASCOGNE, LIMOUSIN, MARCHE, BOURBONNAIS, NIVERNAIS, AUVERGNE, LYONNAIS, FOREZ, BEAUJOLAIS, DAUPHINÉ, PROVENCE, ROUSSILLON, LORRAINE, ALSACE, FRANCHE-COMTÉ, CORSICA, Massif Central, CÉVENNES, VOSGES, JURA, ALPS, PYRÉNÉES

Cities (France): Paris, St-Denis, Versailles, Lille, Roubaix, Tourcoing, Calais, Dunkerque, Boulogne, Amiens, Arras, Reims, Châlons, Troyes, Rouen, Le Havre, Caen, Cherbourg, St-Malo, Rennes, Brest, Quimper, Lorient, Vannes, St-Nazaire, Nantes, Angers, Le Mans, Laval, Tours, Orléans, Chartres, Bourges, Châteauroux, Poitiers, Niort, La Rochelle, Rochefort, Angoulême, Limoges, Périgueux, Bordeaux, Bayonne, Biarritz, Pau, Lourdes, Tarbes, Toulouse, Auch, Montauban, Albi, Rodez, Aurillac, Clermont-Ferrand, Vichy, Moulins, Nevers, Dijon, Chalon, Mâcon, Bourg, Lyon, St-Étienne, Le Puy, Valence, Grenoble, Chambéry, Annecy, Gap, Digne, Nice, Cannes, Grasse, Fréjus, St-Tropez, Toulon, Marseille, Aix-en-Provence, Avignon, Orange, Nîmes, Montpellier, Béziers, Narbonne, Carcassonne, Perpignan, Foix, Mende, Besançon, Belfort, Mulhouse, Colmar, Strasbourg, Metz, Nancy, Épinal, Verdun, Thionville, Charleville, Mézières, Laon, Soissons, Compiègne, Beauvais, Évreux, St-Quentin, Cambrai, Valenciennes, Douai, Béthune, Abbeville

Cities (other countries): Frankfurt, Mannheim, Heidelberg, Karlsruhe, Stuttgart, Freiburg, Basle, Bern, Zürich, Luzern, Neuchâtel, Lausanne, Genève, Torino, Cuneo, Alessandria, Novara, Milano, Monaco, Monte Carlo, San Remo, Bonn, Koblenz, Trier, Luxembourg, Bruxelles, Namur, Charleroi, Liège, Maastricht, Bilbao, San Sebastián, Pamplona, Burgos, Vitoria, Logroño

England: London area — Southampton, Portsmouth, Brighton, Bournemouth, Weymouth, Exeter, Plymouth, Penzance, Land's End, St Ives, Torquay, Dartmouth, Falmouth, Folkestone, Hastings, Newhaven, Chichester, Ryde, Channel Is. (Br.) — Guernsey, Jersey, Alderney, Sark

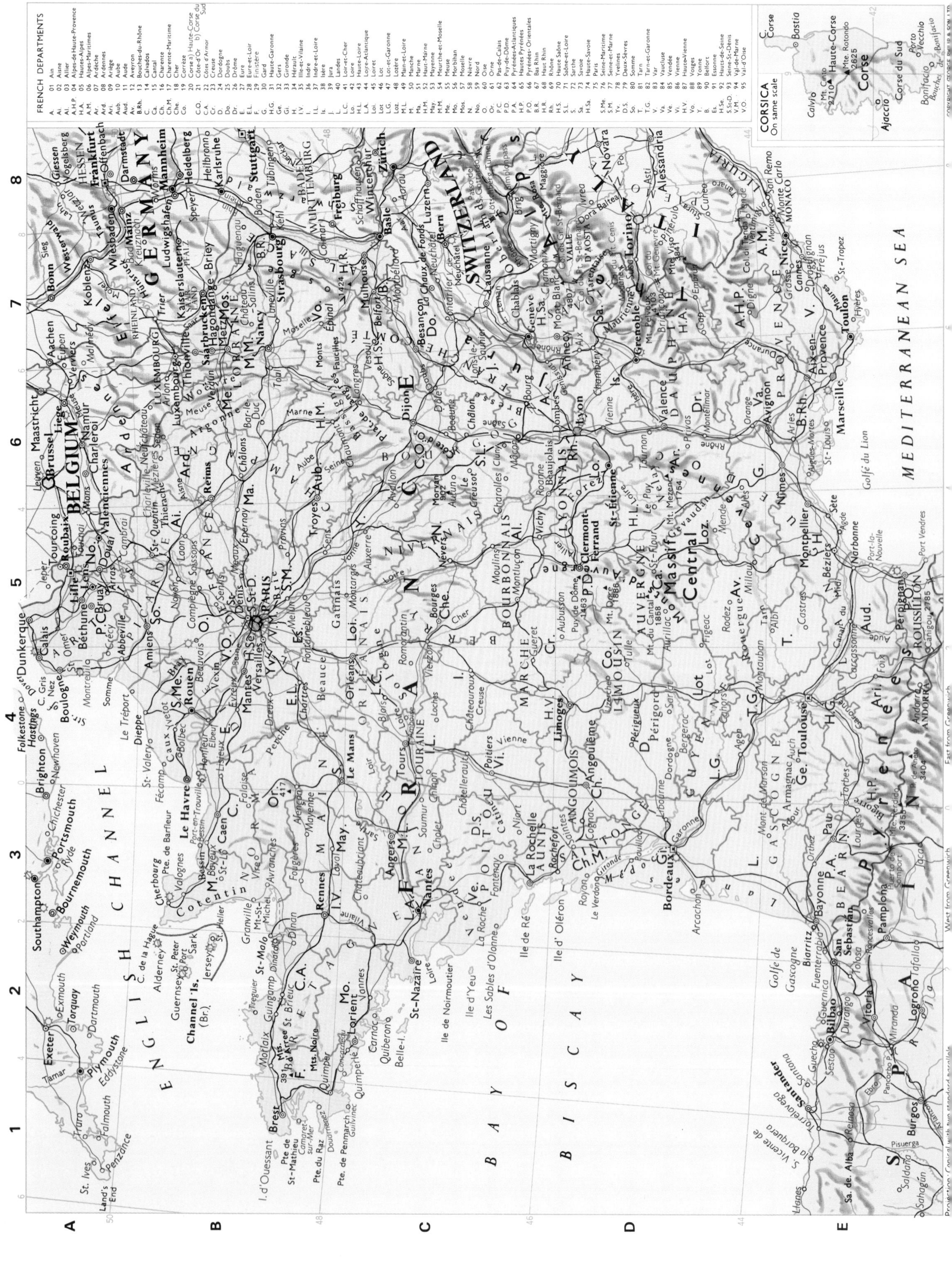

1:5 000 000

100 miles

km

Projection: Conical with two standard parallels

SWITZERLAND

Lyon

FRANCE

Genève

Grenoble

Valence

DAUPHINÉ

Montélimar

Avignon

Orange

PROVENCE

Marseille
Aix
Toulon

Iles d'Hyères

Nice
Cannes
MONACO
Monte Carlo

LIGURIAN SEA

PIEMONTE
Torino (Turin)

Cuneo

Savona
Génova (Genoa)
Riv. di Ponente
Riv. di Levante
Golfo di Génova
La Spézia

Como
Milano (Milan)
Monza
Bergamo
LOMBARDIA
Novara

Pavia
Piacenza
Cremona
Alessandria
Asti
Alba

EMILIA ROMAGNA
Parma
Réggio
Módena
Bologna
Mte. Cimone 2165
Ferrara

Mantova (Mantua)
Verona
Vicenza
Pádova (Padua)
Treviso
Venézia (Venice)
Golfo di Venézia
Chióggia

TRENTINO ALTO ADIGE
Bolzano
Trento
Rovereto
Belluno
Vittório Véneto
VÉNETO

Bressanone
Merano
Ortles 3899
Adamello 3554
Marmolada 3342

FRIULI VENEZIA GIULIA
Udine
Gorízia
Trieste

SLOVENIA
Ljubljana
Klagenfurt
Maribor
Zagreb

CR

Rijeka (Fiume)
Pula (Pola)
Rt. Kamenjak

Cres
Lošinj
Krk

HER

Carrara
Pistóia
Lucca
Pisa
Prato
Firenze (Florence)
Livorno (Leghorn)
TOSCANA
Siena
Arezzo

SAN MARINO
Rímini
Pésaro
Fano
Ancona
Senigállia
MARCHE
Macerata
Ascoli Piceno

Ravenna
Forlì
Cesena

ADRIATIC

Split
Brač
Hvar
Korč
Lastovo
Vis
Šibenik

Capraia
Piombino
Portoferráio
Elba

Mt. Cinto 2710

CORSE (CORSICA) (Fr.)
Ajaccio
Calvi
Bastia
Aléria

Sartene
Pto. Vecchio
Bonifacio
Bouches de Bonifacio

Mare Tirreno

Mte. Argentário
Orbetello
Civitavécchia

Orvieto
Bolsena
Viterbo

UMBRIA
Perúgia
Spoleto 2478
Terni
Rieti

L. Trasimeno
Chiusi
Amiata 1738
Grosseto

ROMA (Rome)
Velletri
Tivoli
Frosinone

ABRUZZI
L'Aquila
Gran Sasso 2914
Pescara
Ortona
Mt. Amaro 2795
Vasto
Térmoli

MOLISE
Campobasso
1056

Asinara
C. Falcone
Golfo dell'Asinara
Porto Torres
Sássari
Alghero
Bosa
Nuoro

SARDEGNA (SARDINIA)
C. Mte. Santo
Mt. Gennargentu 1834

Óbia (Terranova)
Caprera
Golfo Aranci
La Maddalena

2855

Oristano
Golfo di Oristano
Sorgono
Terralba
Iglésias
Carbonia
Portoscuso
G. di Pálmas
C. Spartivento
Cágliari
C. Carbonara
Golfo di Cágliari

3719

TYRRHENIAN SEA

Ánzio
Latina
Gaeta
Terracina
Ísole Ponziane
CAMPANIA
Caserta
Benevento
Avellino
Nocera
Napoli (Naples)
Vesúvio 1277
Torre del Greco
Sorrento
Salerno
Castellammare
Íschia
Cápri

Foggia
G. di Manfredónia
Monte S. Ángelo
Monte Gargano
Cerignola
Andria
Barletta
Trani
Molfetta
PUGLIA
Potenza
Éboli
BASILICATA
Matera
Tàran

3340
Etna

Ustica (It.)

Ísole Eólie o Lípari
Strómboli
Salina
Lípari
Vulcano

C. Peloro
Milazzo
Patti
Messina
Str. di Messina
Réggio
C. Spartivento

Palermo
Trápani
Érice
Castellammare
Ísole Égadi
Favignana
Marsala
Castelvetrano
Selinunte
Sciacca
Menfi
Alcamo
Segesta
SICILIA
Caltanissetta
Enna
Piazza
Caltagirone
Favara
Agrigento
Pto. Empédocle
Licata
Gela
Catánia
Lentini
Augusta
Adrano
Paternò
Giarre
Ferla
Siracusa (Syracuse)
Ragusa
Módica
Noto
Vittória
Comiso
C. Passero

Cosenza
CALABRIA
1929
Crotone
Nicastro
Sambiase
Tauriánova
Pizzo
Palmi
Bagnara

271

Golf Tár

Skikda
C. de Fer
Annaba
Constantine
Khenchela
Tébessa

ALGERIA

Béja
TUNISIA
Binzert (Bizerte)
Tunis
G. de Tunis
C. Bon
Nabeul
G. de Hammamet
Kairouan
Sousse

La Galite

Pantelleria (Ital.)

1730

MEDIT

Lampedusa (Ital.)

Gozo
Comino
Mdina
Valletta
MALTA

RUSSIA
1. Daghestan Rep.
2. Kabardino–Balkar Rep.
3. Mari Rep.
4. Mordovian Rep.
5. North Ossetian Rep.
6. Tatar Rep.
7. Udmurt Rep.
8. Chuvash Rep.
9. Checheno–Ingush Rep.
AZERBAIJAN
10. Nakhichevan Rep.
GEORGIA
11. Abkhaz Rep.
12. Adzhar Rep.

Projection: Conical Orthomorphic with two standard parallels

East from Greenwich

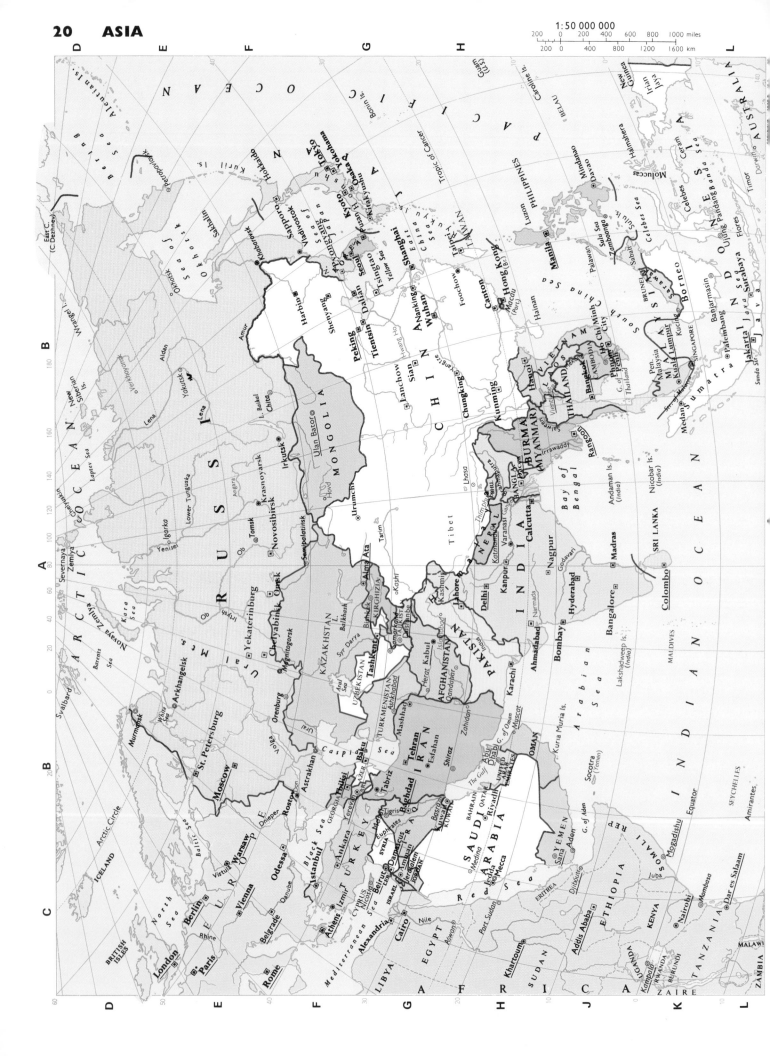

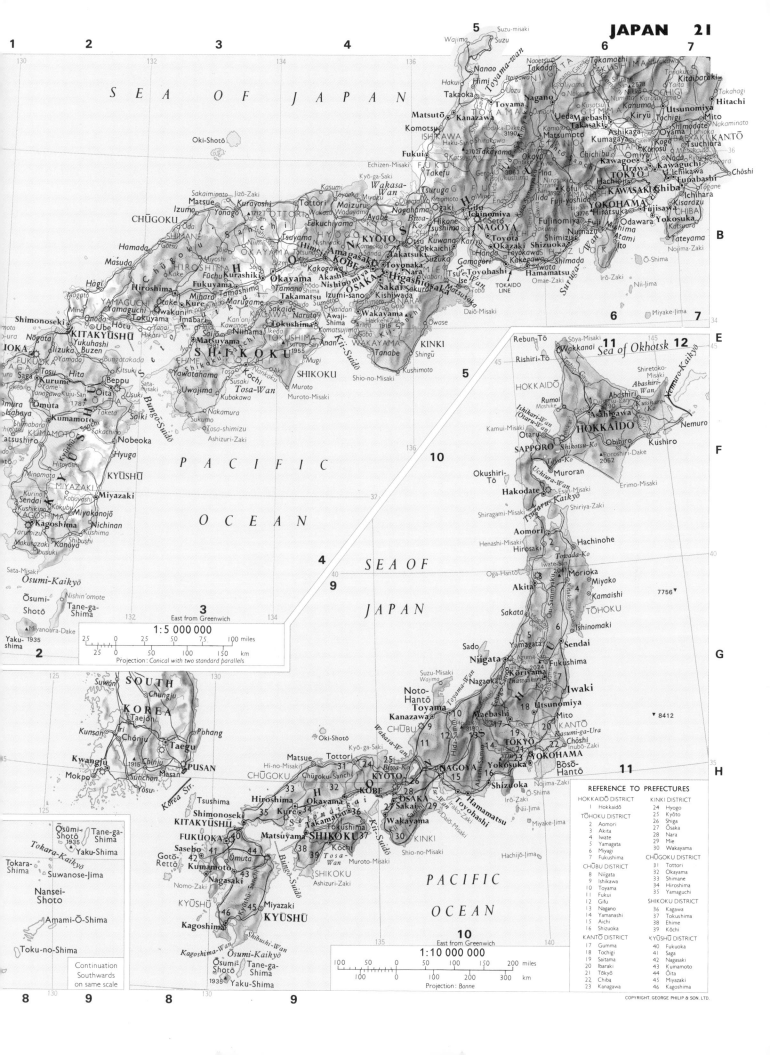

1:20 000 000

| 100 | 0 | 100 | 200 | 300 | 400 miles |
| 100 | 0 | 100 | 200 | 300 | 400 | 500 | 600 km |

RUSSIA

KAZAKHSTAN

KIRGHIZIA

MONGOLIA

Ulaanbaatar (Ulan Bator)

CHINA

XINJIANG UYGUR

Tarim Pendi

Dzungaria Pendi

Urumqi (Wulumqi)

Kunlun Shan

Altun Shan

Qilian Shan

QINGHAI

XIZANG (TIBET)

Lhasa

NEPAL

Katmandu

BHUTAN

BANGLADESH

Dhaka

INDIA

CALCUTTA

BAY OF BENGAL

MYANMAR (BURMA)

Mandalay

LAOS

THAILAND

VIETNAM

HANOI

Haiphong

G. of Tonkin

Hainan Dao

HAINAN

SOUTH CHINA SEA

PHILIPPINES

Luzon

TAIWAN (FORMOSA)

Taibei

Gaoxiong

Bashi Channel

Batan Is.

Hong Kong

Macao

GUANGZHOU

Kowloon

Shantou

GUANGDONG

GUANGXI

Nanning

Guilin

Zhanjiang

Beihai

YUNNAN

Kunming

GUIZHOU

Guiyang

SICHUAN

CHENGDU

CHONGQING

Daxue Shan

Bayan Har Shan

Hoh Xil Shan

Tanggula Shan

Nyainqentanglha Shan

Brahmaputra

ASSAM

RYUKYU-RETTO

Okinawa

Sakishima-Gunto

Tropic of Cancer

EAST CHINA SEA

JAPAN

Fukuoka

Sasebo

Nagasaki

SOUTH KOREA

Pusan

Taegu

Kwangju

Mokpo

Cheju

Cheju Do

Inch'on

Taejon

Chonju

NORTH KOREA

Pyongyang

Hungnam

Korea Bay

Korea Str.

Tsushima

YELLOW SEA

DALIAN

Yantai

Qingdao

Weifang

SHANDONG

Jinan

Zibo

Bo Hai

TIANJIN

BEIJING

Tangshan

Chengde

Zhangjiakou

Datong

Hohhot

BAOTOU

Yinchuan

NINGXIA

Lanzhou

XI'AN

Baoji

Qin Ling

SHAANXI

GANSU

SHANXI

TAIYUAN

Shijiazhuang

HEBEI

HENAN

Zhengzhou

Luoyang

Kaifeng

Xuzhou

Huai

JIANGSU

NANJING

SHANGHAI

Wuxi

Suzhou

Hangzhou

ZHEJIANG

Ningbo

Wenzhou

ANHUI

Hefei

Bengbu

WUHAN

HUBEI

Yichang

HUNAN

Changsha

Hengyang

Xiangtan

JIANGXI

Nanchang

Jiujiang

FUJIAN

Fuzhou

Xiamen

Quanzhou

Chang (Yangtze)

Huang (Yellow R.)

HEILONGJIANG

HARBIN

Qiqihar

Daqing

Mudanjiang

Jiamusi

Hegang

Hailar

Da Hinggan Ling

Xiao Hinggan Ling

JILIN

Changchun

Jilin

Siping

LIAONING

SHENYANG

Anshan

Fushun

Benxi

Liaoyang

Dandong

Jinzhou

Yingkou

Vladivostok

Khabarovsk

Ozero Baikal

Irkutsk

Ulan Ude

Chita

Semipalatinsk

Karaganda

Ozero Balkhash

Alma Ata

Bishkek

JAMMU & KASHMIR

KARAKORAM

Lucknow

Varanasi

Allahabad

Patna

Kanpur

1:20 000 000

100   0   100   200   300   400   500 miles
100   0   200   400   600   800 km

PACIFIC OCEAN

BELAU

IRIAN JAYA

Equator

Supiori
Yapen
Monokwari
Cenderawasih
Waigeo
Sorong
Jazirah Doberai
Wasior
Wokam
Kobroor
Trangan
Aru
Teluk Barau
Fakfak
Misool
Gebe
Kepulauan
SERAM SEA
Seram
Ambon
Buru
Namlea
Mangole
Taliabu
Peleng
Banggai
BANDA SEA
Kepulauan
Banda
Wessel Is.
C. Arnhem
ARAFURA SEA
Melville I.
Van Diemen
Bathurst I.
Darwin
AUSTRALIA

TAIWAN (FORMOSA)
Bashi Channel
Batan Is.
Babuyan Chan.
Babuyan Is.
Aparri
Laoag
LUZON
2928 Baguio
Dagupan
Quezon City
MANILA
Manila B.
Batangas
Catanduanes
Polillo Islands
Lagonoy G.
Sorsogon
S. Bernardino Str.
Samar
Masbate
Tacloban
Ormoc
Leyte
Buyan
Cagayan
Surigao Strait
Davao
C. S. Agustin
Davao Gulf
Mindanao
2965
Moro Gulf
Zamboanga
Basilan
Jolo
Sulu Arch.
Tinaca Point
Sarangani B.
Palau
Sangihe
Talaud
Kepulauan
Morotai
Halmahera
Ternate
Manado
Gorontalo
Teluk Tomini
SULAWESI (CELEBES)
Kendari
Butung
Rantepao
3455
Salajar
Ujung Pandang (Makasar)
Kepulauan
Bonerate
FLORES SEA
Flores
Sumbawa
3726
Lombok
Bali
Sumba
Sawu
Sawu Sea
TIMOR
Kupang
Dili
Wetar
Alor
Pantar
Lomblen
Ruteng
Nusa Tenggara (Lesser Sunda Islands)
TIMOR SEA
Waingapu
Yamdena
Tanimbar
Kai
Seru
Selaru

PHILIPPINE SEA
Calamian
Group
Mindoro
Mindoro Str.
Calapan
Panay
Iloilo
Negros
Bacolod
Cebu
Bohol
Ozamiz
SULU SEA
Palawan
Balabac Str.
Banggi
Kudat
Kota Kinabalu (Jesselton)
4101
SABAH
Labuan
Pulau Labuan
Victoria
BRUNEI
Miri
SARAWAK
Sibu
Kuching

CELEBES SEA
Tarakan
Tawau
Sibuko B.
Parket B.
Selat Makasar
Samarinda
Balikpapan
BORNEO
KALIMANTAN
Pegunungan Muller
Pegunungan Schwaner
Banjarmasin
Barito

HONG KONG (Br.)
Macau (Port.)
Zhanjiang
Hainan
Haikou
Beihai
Haiphong
Hanoi
CHINA

SOUTH CHINA SEA
Paracel Is.
Spratly
Amboyna
Con Son
Kepulauan Natuna Besar
Kepulauan Anambas
Natuna Selatan
Kepulauan Tambelan
Pulau Bunguran

Da Nang (Tourane)
An Nhon
Qui Nhon
Nha Trang
Phan Rang
Phan Thiet
PHANH BHO HO CHI MINH (Saigon)
Go Cong
Ca Mau
VIET-NAM
Hué
Quang Tri
Thanh Hoa
Vinh
LAOS
Vientiane
Savannakhet
Pakse
CAMBODIA
PHNOM PENH
Tonle Sap
Battambang
Kratie
THAILAND (SIAM)
BANGKOK
Ayutthaya
Nakhon Ratchasima (Khorat)
Chanthaburi
Phnom Dangrek
Gulf of Thailand

BURMA (MYANMAR)
RANGOON
Bassein
Pye
Toungoo
Moulmein
Amherst
Tavoy
Mergui
Myeik
G. of Martaban

ANDAMAN SEA
Andaman Islands
Middle Andaman
Little Andaman
Pt. Blair
Ten Degree Channel
Car Nicobar
Nicobar Islands (India)
Great Nicobar

Phuket
Nakhon Si Thammarat
Songkhla
Trang
Kota Baharu
Kuala Terengganu
George Town
Penang
Butterworth
Taiping
Ipoh
MALAYSIA
Kuala Lumpur
Port Kelang
Seremban
Malacca
Muar
Johor Baharu
SINGAPORE
Selat Malacca

Kepulauan Riau
Kepulauan Lingga
Kepulauan Bangka
Bangka
Pangkalpinang
Palembang
Pulau Belitung
Kepulauan Karimata

SUMATRA
Banda Aceh (Kutaraja)
Medan
Pematangsiantar
Tebingtinggi
Padang
Bukittinggi
Sawahlunto
Pekanbaru
Jambi
Danau Toba
Nias
Siberut
Kepulauan Mentawai
Enggano

Pontianak
Kapuas

JAKARTA
Bogor
BANDUNG
Cirebon
Tegal
Pekalongan
Semarang
SURABAYA
Madiun
Kediri
Malang
Yogyakarta
Surakarta
Magelang
JAVA
Greater Sunda Islands
Madura
Bawean
Kepulauan Kangean
MOLUCCA SEA
Moluccas

INDIAN OCEAN
Christmas I. (Austral.)
Cocos or Keeling Is. (Austral.)

East from Greenwich
Equator

Projection: Bonne

1:20 000 000

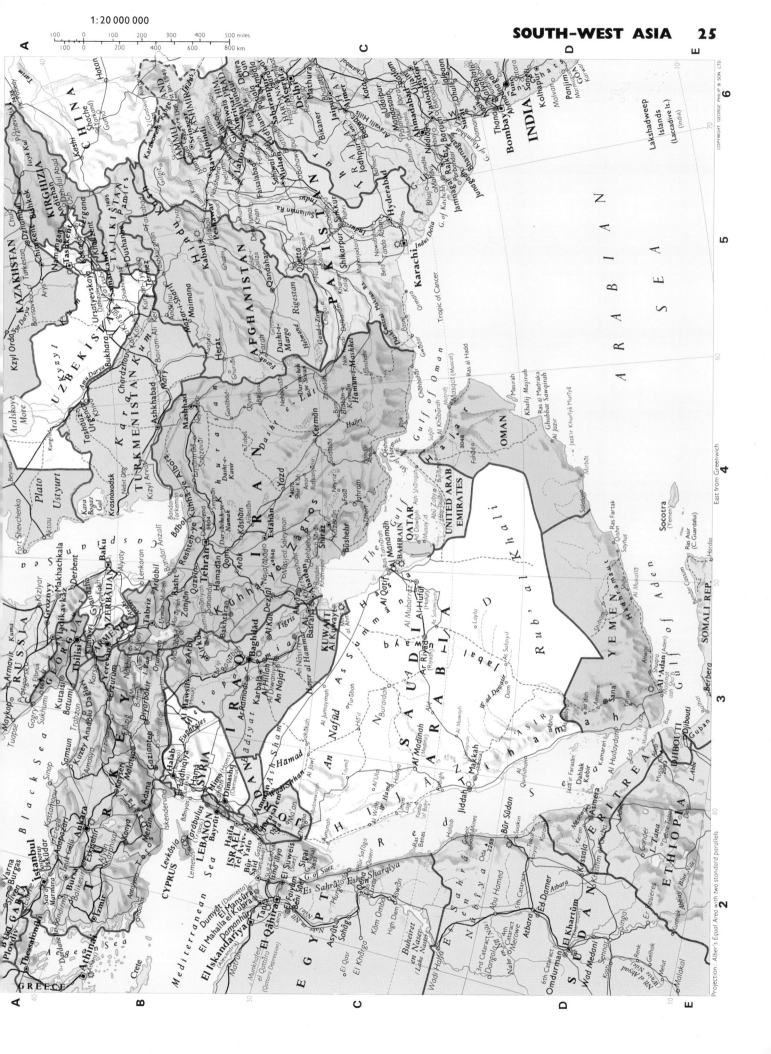

1:20 000 000

COPYRIGHT GEORGE PHILIP & SON LTD

Projection: Alber's Equal Area with two standard parallels

A B C D E F G H

1 2 3 4 5 6

NORTH ATLANTIC

OCEAN

▼ 6578

Cabo de São Vicente

Cádiz **SPAIN** ○Málaga ○Almería

Str. of Gibraltar Gibraltar (Br.) Ceuta (Sp.) Melilla

Tanger Tetouan Al Hoceima

Larache El Rif Oujda

Ksar el Kebir Quezzane Taza Jerada El Aricha

Kenitra (Port Lyautey) Fès Tlemcen

Salé Meknès Moyen Atlas

Rabat Khouribga Bou Arfa Figuig

Casablanca Berrechid

El Jadida Settat Ar Rachidya

Safi Marrakech Beni Mellal Beni Ounif

Essaouira Ouarzazate Béchar Abadla

C. Rhir 4166 Taroudannt Ig Beni Abbès

Agadir Anti Atlas Dra Kerzaz

Madeira (Port.) Pto. Santo Funchal

Ifni Tiznit Mengoub Charouine Timimoun

Islas Canarias (Sp.) Lanzarote Arrecife

La Palma Fuerteventura Puerto del Rosario

Tenerife Sta. Cruz Gran Canaria Las Palmas

Gomera C. Juby Tarfaya (Villa Bens) Tindouf

Hierro El Aaiún Semara

ALGERIA

Plateau du Tademaït

Bj. Fly Ste. Marie Adrar In Belbel In Salah

Zaouiet Reggane Aoulef el Arab

C. Bojador Bu Craa Chegga Arak

WESTERN SAHARA

Ain Ben Tili Er Chech Ouallene

Bir Mogrein

Dakhla Pta. Durnford

C. Barbas Fdérik Zouérate Terhazza Tanezrouft

Taoudenni Poste Maurice Cortier (Bidon 5)

Nouâdhibou (Port Étienne) Chår

Ras Nouâdhibou La Güera Atâr Ouadâne

Oujeft Chinguetti Adrar des Iforhas

Akjoujt Tessalit

C. Timiris Rachid Tichit Mabrouk

Nouakchott Moudjéria Akreijit

Boutilimit Tâmchekket Araouane Kidal

Mederdra Meg Ouâlâta Bou Djébéha

Bogué Kiffa Tombouctou Bamba Kerchoual

St. Louis Podor Sélibabi Néma Goundam Bourem

Rosso Dagana Timbedgha Niafouké Diré Gourma-Rharous Gao

Louga Kaédi Nioro du Sahel Bossikounou Hombori Ansongo Ménaka

Tivaouane Linguère Mbout Nara Agadez

Thiès Diourbel Matam Yélimané Douentza

SENEGAL Tiel Sokolo Mopti Djibo Téra Filingué

Kaffrine Tambacounda Bakel Mourdiah Didiéni Sofara Bandiagara Dori Tillabéri Niamey Dosso

GAMBIA Kayes Kita Ségou Djenné Ouahigouya Kaya Birni Nkonni

Banjul Georgetown Gambia Satadougou Kolokani Sarro Douentza **BURKINA FASO**

Sédhiou Kédougou Bamako Koulikoro San Séné Ouagadougou Gaya Sokoto

GUINEA-BISSAU Fouta Djalon Tougué Siguiri Bougouni Sikasso Koutiala Koudougou Tenkodogo Kande

Bissau Gaoual Dinguiraye Kankan Bobo-Dioulasso Léo **BENIN** Zaria

Arquipélago dos Bijagós Boké Télimélé Pita Dabola Kouroussa Banfora Diébougou Gaoua Tumu **TOGO** Kaduna

C. Verga Dubréka Kindia Faranah Kissidougou Odienné Korhogo **IVORY COAST** Tamale **NIGERIA**

Conakry **SIERRA LEONE** Beyla Touba Mankono Bouaké Kumasi **GHANA** Lomé Lagos

Freetown Makeni Séguéla Lake Volta **BENIN CITY**

LEONE Bo Man Danané Daloa Bondoukou Abomey Porto-Novo Cotonou

Sherbro Kenema Toulépleu Guiglo Yamoussoukro Sekondi-Takoradi Onitsha

Monrovia **LIBERIA** Tapeta Gagnoa Cape Coast Accra Tema Port-Harcourt Aba

Marshall Buchanan Greenville Abidjan Grand Bassam **Bight of Benin** Bioko Douala

River Cess C. Palmas Tabou San-Pédro C. Three Points Mont Cameroun 4070 **CAM**

NIGER

MALI

MAURITANIA El Djouf

Ahaggar Tahat 2918 Tamanrasset

Adrar Air (Azbine) Monts Tarraga Iferouâne Agadez

ALGER (Algiers) El Harrach Blida Médéa Constantine Sétif Batna Annaba Skikda Béjaïa Tizi-Ouzou

Ech Cheliff Mostaganem Oran Sidi-Bel-Abbès Mascara Tiaret Djelfa Laghouat Ghardaïa Ouargla Hassi Messaoud El Oued

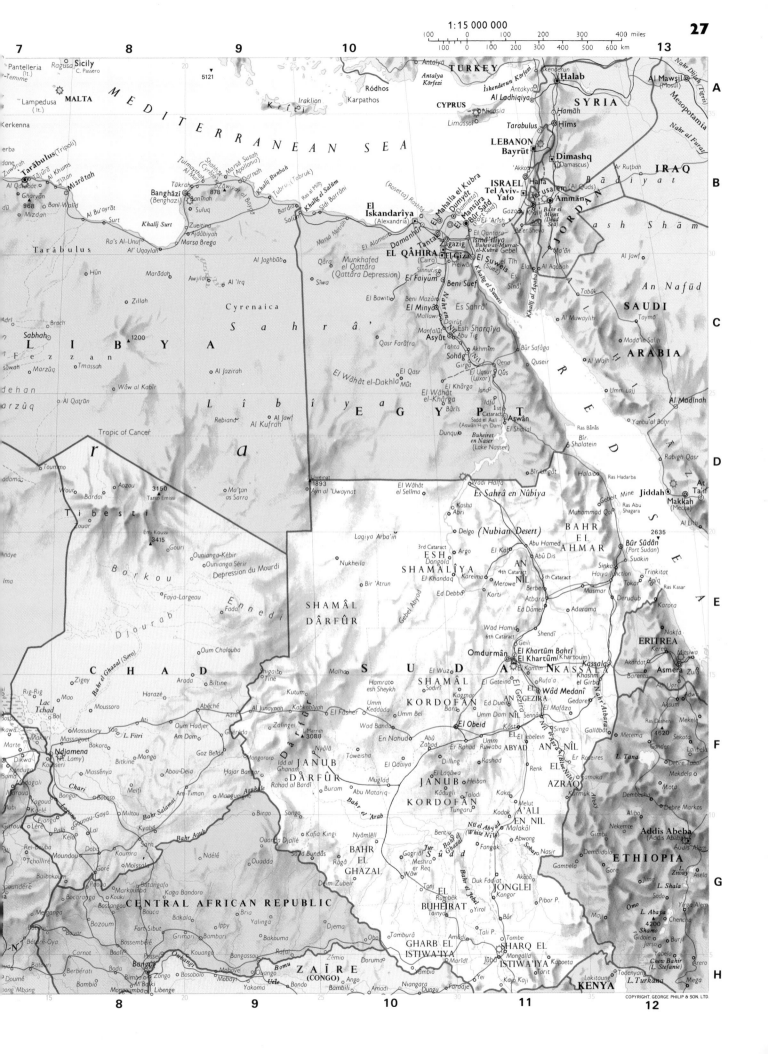

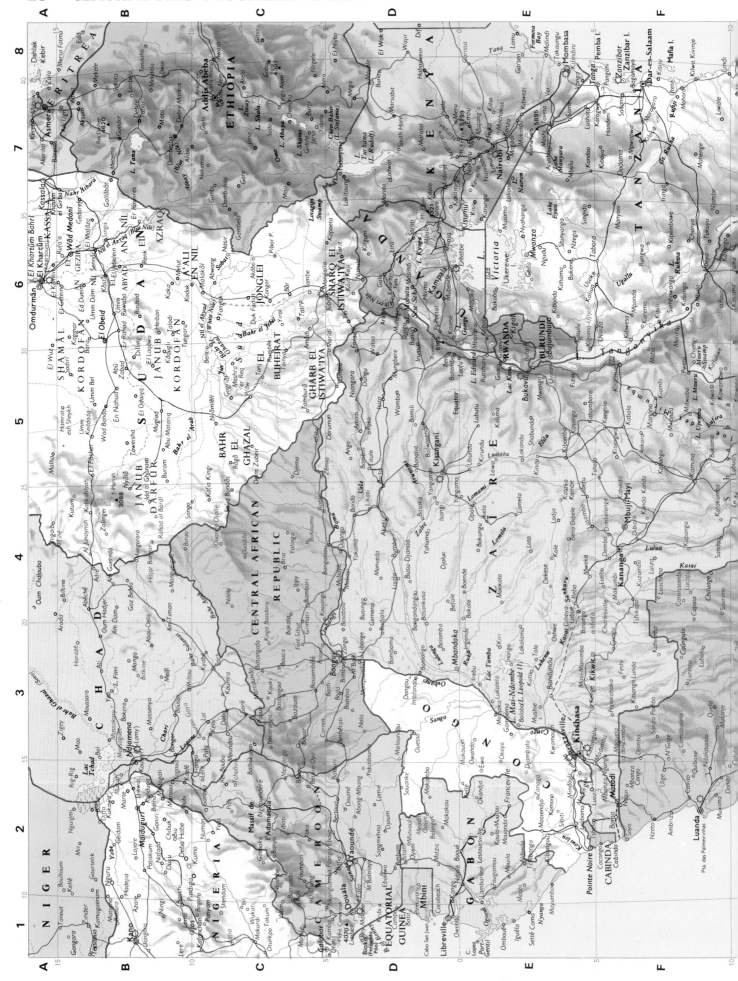

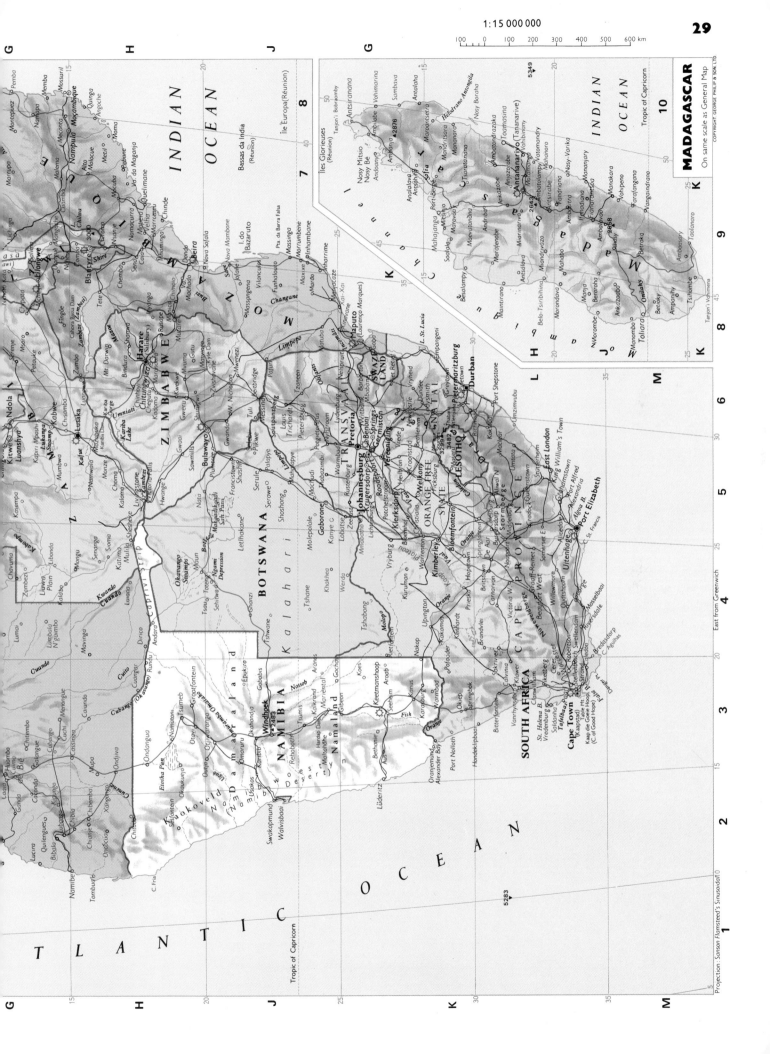

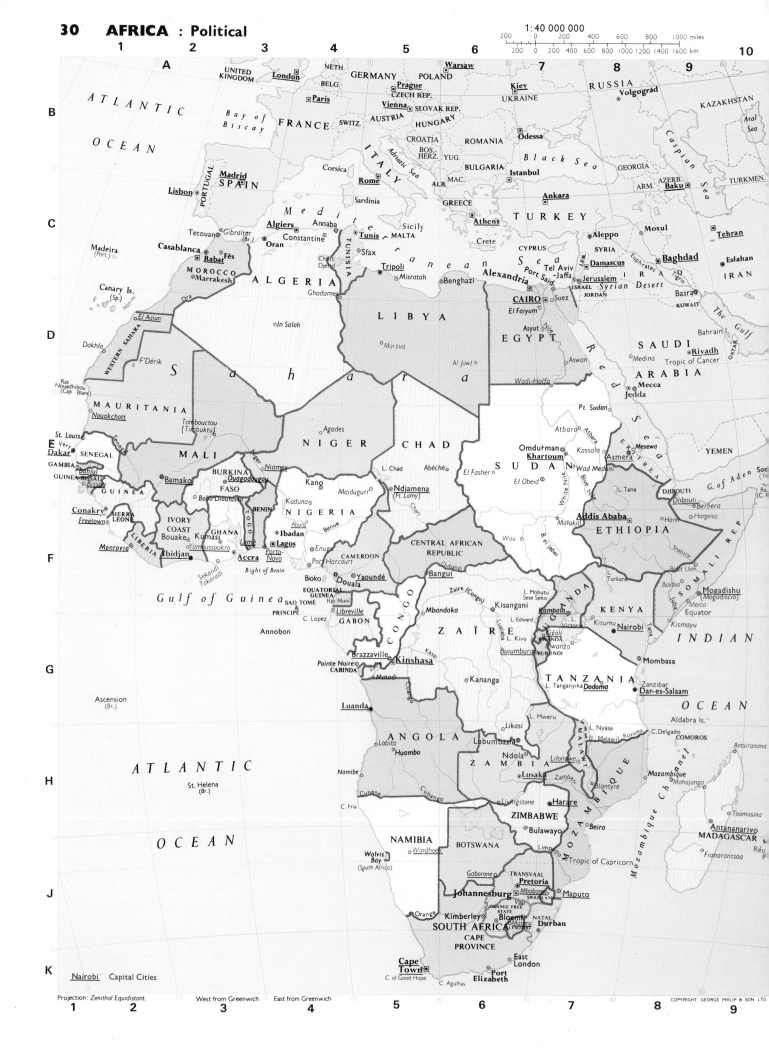

1:40 000 000

200 0 200 400 600 800 1000 miles
200 0 200 400 600 800 1000 1200 1400 1600 km

A

1 **2** **3** **4** **5** **6** **7** **8** **9** **10**

UNITED
KINGDOM
□ London
NETH.
GERMANY
POLAND
□ Warsaw
RUSSIA
□ Kiev Volgograd
UKRAINE
KAZAKHSTAN

B

A T L A N T I C

Bay of
Biscay
FRANCE
SWITZ.
AUSTRIA
HUNGARY
CROATIA
BOS.-HERZ.
YUG.
ROMANIA
□ Odessa
Black Sea
GEORGIA
Aral
Sea
Caspian
Sea

O C E A N

□ Paris
BELG.
□ Prague
CZECH REP.
□ Vienna □ SLOVAK REP.
BULGARIA
□ Istanbul
ARM.
AZERB. □ Baku
TURKMEN.

C

Madeira
(Port.)
PORTUGAL
□ Madrid
SPAIN
Corsica
ITALY
□ Rome
Sardinia
Adriatic Sea
ALB.
MAC.
GREECE
□ Athens
TURKEY
□ Ankara
□ Aleppo
SYRIA
CYPRUS
Mosul
□ Tehran

□ Lisbon
□ Algiers
Annaba
Constantine
Sfax
□ Tunis MALTA
Crete
Mediterranean
Sea
□ Damascus
LEB.
□ Baghdad
Esfahan
IRAN

Tetouan
Gibraltar
(Br.)
□ Casablanca Fès
□ Rabat
Oran
TUNISIA
Tripoli
Misratah
Benghazi
Alexandria
Port Said
Tel Aviv-Jaffa
ISRAEL □ Jerusalem
Syrian Desert
JORDAN
Basra
IRAQ
KUWAIT

D

Canary Is.
(Sp.)
MOROCCO
Marrakesh
ALGERIA
Ghadames
In Salah
L I B Y A
Marzuq
Al Jawf
CAIRO
El Faiyum
Suez
Asyut
EGYPT
Nile
Aswan
Wadi-Halfa
Medina
SAUDI
□ Riyadh
Tropic of Cancer
Bahrain
QATAR
The Gulf

Dakhla
WESTERN SAHARA
F'Dérik
Dra
S a h a r a
Mecca
Jedda
ARABIA

E

Ras
Nouadhibou
(Cap Blanc)
MAURITANIA
□ Nouakchott
Tombouctou
(Timbuktu)
Agades
NIGER
CHAD
Abéché
El Fasher
SUDAN
□ Khartoum
Omdurman
Atbara
Atbara
Kassala
Wad Medani
□ Asmera
Mesewa
ERITREA
YEMEN

St. Louis
C. Vert
□ Dakar SENEGAL
MALI
□ Bamako
Niger
Niamey
Kano
L. Chad
Ndjamena
(Ft. Lamy)
Maiduguri
El Obeid
White Nile
Blue Nile
L. Tana
DJIBOUTI
Djibouti
G. of Aden
Berbera
GAMBIA
□ Banjul
GUINEA-BISSAU
□ Bissau
BURKINA
FASO
□ Ouagadougou
Bobo-Dioulasso
Kaduna
NIGERIA
□ Abuja
Ibadan
Benue
Wau
B. el Jebel
Wau
Malakal
□ Addis Ababa
Harer
ETHIOPIA
Hargeisa

F

Conakry
GUINEA
Freetown
SIERRA
LEONE
IVORY
COAST
Kumasi
Bouaké
GHANA
Yamoussoukro
Lomé
TOGO
BENIN
Porto-Novo
□ Lagos
Enugu
Port Harcourt
CAMEROON
□ Yaoundé
Douala
CENTRAL AFRICAN
REPUBLIC
□ Bangui
Oubangui
Zaïre (Congo)
Kisangani
UGANDA
L. Mobutu
Sese Seko
L. Turkana
SOMALI REP.
Belet Uen
Baidoa
□ Mogadishu
(Mogadiscio)
Merca

Monrovia
LIBERIA
□ Abidjan
Sekondi
Takoradi
Bight of Benin
Bioko
EQUATORIAL
GUINEA
Rio Muni
SAO TOMÉ
& PRINCIPE
□ Libreville
C. Lopez
GABON
CONGO
Mbandaka
Z A Ï R E
L. Edward
L. Kivu
RWANDA
□ Kigali
BURUNDI
□ Bujumbura
Mwanza
L. Victoria
□ Kampala
Kisumu
KENYA
□ Nairobi
Mombasa
Equator
Kismayu
INDIAN

G

Ascension
(Br.)
Gulf of Guinea
Annobon
Brazzaville
Pointe Noire
CABINDA
□ Kinshasa
Matadi
Kasai
Kananga
Luanda
Lulua
L. Tanganyika
T A N Z A N I A
□ Dodoma
□ Dar-es-Salaam
Zanzibar
O C E A N

H

A T L A N T I C
St. Helena
(Br.)
Namibe
Likasi
Lobito
Huambo
A N G O L A
Lubumbashi
Ndola°
ZAMBIA
□ Lusaka
Cunene
Cubango
L. Mweru
L. Nyasa
(L. Malawi)
Lilongwe
Ruvuma
C. Delgado
COMOROS
Antsiranana
Mahajanga
Mozambique
MALAWI
Blantyre
MOZAMBIQUE
Beira
Zambezi
Toamasina
MADAGASCAR
Antananarivo
Mozambique Channel

O C E A N
C. Fria
NAMIBIA
Livingstone
□ Harare
ZIMBABWE
Bulawayo
BOTSWANA
Limpopo
Tropic of Capricorn
Fianarantsoa

J

Walvis
Bay
(South Africa)
□ Windhoek
Gaborone
TRANSVAAL
□ Pretoria
Johannesburg
□ Mbabane
SWAZILAND
□ Maputo

Orange
Kimberley
ORANGE FREE
STATE
□ Bloemfontein
□ Maseru
LESOTHO
NATAL
Durban
SOUTH AFRICA
CAPE
PROVINCE
Vaal

K

□ Nairobi Capital Cities

□ Cape
Town
C. of Good Hope
C. Agulhas
East
London
□ Port
Elizabeth

Projection: Zenithal Equidistant.
West from Greenwich
East from Greenwich
COPYRIGHT. GEORGE PHILIP & SON, LTD

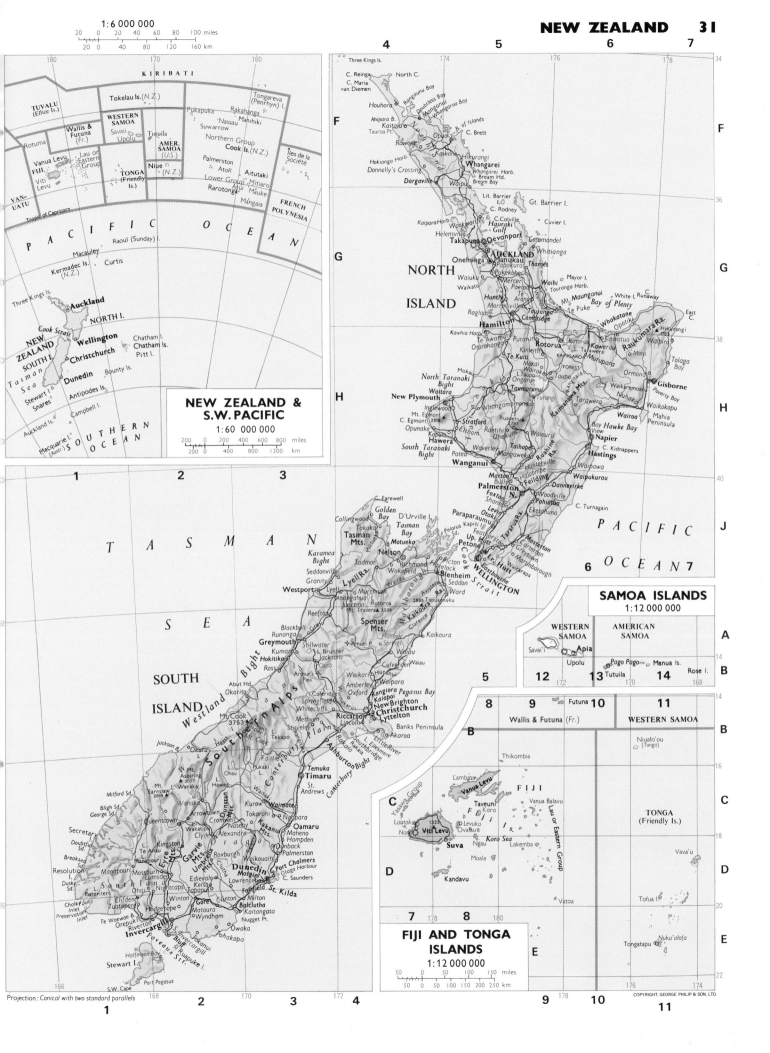

1:6 000 000

NEW ZEALAND & S.W. PACIFIC
1:60 000 000

SAMOA ISLANDS
1:12 000 000

WESTERN SAMOA   AMERICAN SAMOA

FIJI AND TONGA ISLANDS
1:12 000 000

Projection: Conical with two standard parallels

COPYRIGHT. GEORGE PHILIP & SON. LTD.

1   2   3   4   130   5

115   120   125

A

J a v a   T r e n c h   ▼6389

Croker
Dundas   Cobourg Pen.
Bathurst I.   Melville I.   Goulburn Is.   Junction B.
Van 'Diemen   Crocodile
Clarence Str.   Gulf
P. Darwin   Castlereagh B.
Darwin   Buckingham

Ashmore Reef   Cartier I.
C. Londonderry
C. Talbot
Vansittart B.
C. Bougainville   Admiralty G.
Bonaparte   Montague Sd.
Archipelago
York. Sd.
Brunswick B.

Pt. Blaze   Anson B.
Rum Jungle
C. Ford   Batchelor
Jos. Bonaparte   Frances Creek
Gulf   Pine Creek
Arnhem Land

Scott Reef
Drysdale
Cambridge G.
Queens Chan.
Katherine   Roper
Matharanka

T I M O R   S E A

Koolan & Cockatoo Is.
C. Lévêque
Lacepede Is.
King Sd.
Yampi Sound
Mt. Hann 776▲
L. Argyle
Kununurra
Wyndham   Gulf Basin   Victoria
Daly
Birdum
Larrimah
Daly Waters

15

Rowley Shoals
C. Baskerville
Carnot B.
C. Boileau
Derby   Meda
Broome
King Leopold Ras.   Mt. Ord
936   Glenroy
Durack Range
K i m b e r l e y
Victoria River Downs
Wave Hill   Newcastle Waters
L. Woods
Powell Creek   Renner Springs T
Bar

Roebuck B.
C. Latouche Treville
C. Bossut
La Grange
Dampier Downs
Fitzroy
Fitzroy Crossing
Hall's Creek
GREAT NORTHERN
Gordon Downs
Sturt

B

N O R T H E
T E R R I T

Eighty Mile Beach
C a n n i n g   B a s i n
Gregory Lake
Hordern Hills
The Granites
Murchison Ra.
Daver Ra.

Dampier Archipelago
Finucane   P. Hedland   Mount Goldsworthy
De Grey
G r e a t   S a n d y   D e s e r t
Mt. Singleton
▲844
Mt. Freeling
998   Barrow Creek T.O.
San

20

HamptonHarb.
Monte Bello Is.
Barrow I.   C. Preston
Dampier
Roebourne
Pilbara
Nimingarra
Marble Bar
Throssell Ra.   L. Blanche
Nullagine
L. Dora
L. Mackay
Reynolds Ra.
Mt. Ziel 1510
Mt. Liebig 1524
L. Macdonald
Mt. Laughl
1169
Alice Springs

N.W. Cape
Exmouth G.
Learmonth
Pt. Cloates
Deepdale
Onslow
Mt. Enid
Hamersley Ra.
Fortescue
Wittenoom
Shaw
Yule
Mt. Nicholas
Robertson Ra.
Newman
L. Disappointment
G i b s o n   D e s e r t
Rawlinson Ra.
L. Amadeus
Mt. Olga 1069
Ayers Rock 867
Macdonnell Ras.
James Ra.
Palmer   Hugh
Finke

C

C. Farquhar
L. McLeod
C. Cuvier
Geographe Chan.
Bernier
Dorre I.
Tom Price 1227
Ophthalmia Ra.
1251
Mt. Bruce
Mt. Meharry
Ashburton
Mount Whaleback
Parraburdoo
W E S T E R N
Barlee Ra.
Mt. Augustus ▲1105
Mt. Egerton 994
L. Buchanan
Blackstone Ra.
Barrow Ra.
M u s g r a v e   R a n g e s   1440
Mt. Woodroffe
Everard Ras.
Hamilton
Alberga
Oodnadat

25

Naturaliste Chan.
Dirk Hartog
Denham
S. Passage
Steep Pt.
Shark B.
Carnarvon
Gascoyne
Wooramel
North West Basin
Murchison
Robinson
Peak Hill
Ras.
L. Carnegie
L. Wells ▲661
L. Yeo
G r e a t   V i c t o r i a   D e s e r t
Cooper Pedy

D

Gantheaume B.
P. Gregory
Houtman
Abrolhos
Northampton
Champion B.
Geraldton
Dongara
Mullewa
Yalgoo
Sanford
Meekatharra
Nannine
Cue
L. Austin
Sandstone
Mt. Magnet
Tallering Peak ▲453
L. Barlee
L. Monger
L. Moore
Leonora
Malcolm
L. Carey
L. Raeside
Menzies
L. Ballard
Laverton
L. Rason
L. Minigwal
A U S T R A L I A
Maurice
Maralinga
Oodea
Tarcoola
L. Harris
L. Everard
S O U T H   A U

30

Wiluna

Jurien B.
Wedge I.
Coastal
Plains
Basin
Bonnie Rock
Bencubbin
Bullfinch
Kanowna
Kalgoorlie-Boulder
Coolgardie
Southern Cross
Zanthus
Premier Downs
Rawlinna
Forrest
Deakin
Eucla Basin
N u l l a r b o r   P l a i n
Hampton Tableland
Eyre
Head of Bight
C. Adieu
Fowlers B.
Penong
Ceduna   L. Gairdn
Nuyts Archipelago
C. Radstock
Streaky B.
Anxious B.

Midland
Swan
York
Geraldton
Northam
Merredin
Kellerberrin
Beverley
Brookton
Narrogin
The Johnston Lakes
L. Lefroy
L. Cowan
Norseman
L. Dundas
Pt. Dover
Pt. Culver
Rocky Pt.
G r e a t   A u s t r a l i a n   B i g h t
Investigator Group
Coffin B. Penin.
Whidbey Is.
Port Li

Perth
Fremantle
Kwinana
Pinjarra
Bunbury
Collie
Geographe B.
C. Naturaliste
Busselton
Augusta
C. Leeuwin
Albany
Bridgetown
Manjimup
Pemberton
Mt. Barker
Stirling Ra.
Gnowangerup
Newdegate
Ravensthorpe
Hopetoun
Esperance
C. Pasley
C. Arid
Archipelago of the Recherche
C. le Grand
Doubtful B.
Esperance B.
Pt. Hood
C. Knob

E

I N D I A N   O C E A N

Geographe Chan.
Flinders B.
Pt. d'Entrecasteaux
Pt. Nuyts
Denmark
Tor B.
King George Sound

F

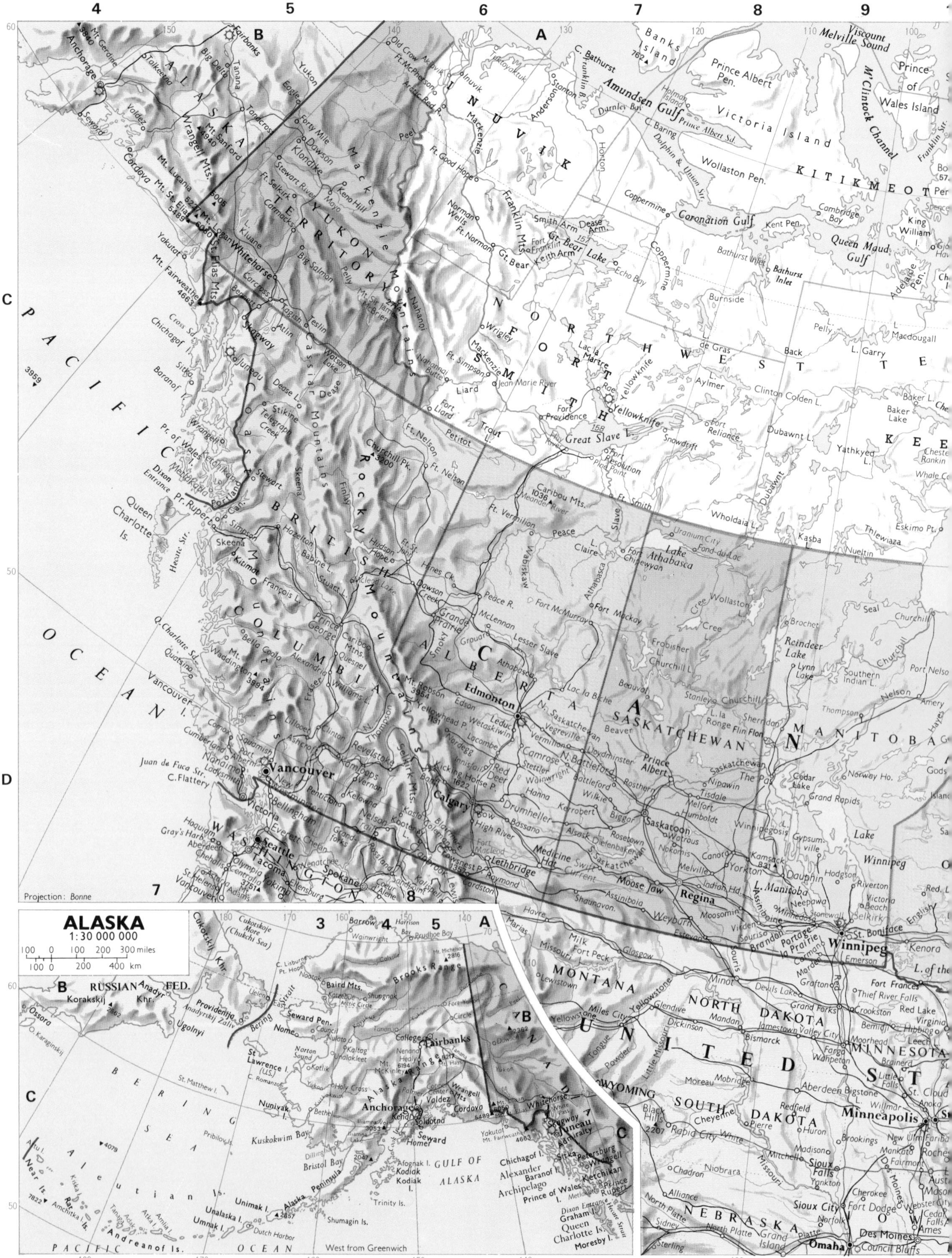

4
5
6
7
8
9
A
B
C
D
PACIFIC
OCEAN
ALASKA
YUKON TERRITORY
INUVIK
KITIKMEOT
KEEWATIN
NORTHWEST TERRITORIES
FORT SMITH
BRITISH COLUMBIA
ALBERTA
SASKATCHEWAN
MANITOBA
WASHINGTON
MONTANA
NORTH DAKOTA
SOUTH DAKOTA
MINNESOTA
NEBRASKA
WYOMING
UNITED STATES
Banks Island
Prince Albert Pen.
Victoria Island
Amundsen Gulf
Viscount Melville Sound
M'Clintock Channel
Prince of Wales Island
Wollaston Pen.
Coronation Gulf
Queen Maud Gulf
Great Bear Lake
Great Slave L.
Lake Athabasca
Mackenzie Mountains
Rocky Mountains
Coast Mountains
Cassiar Mountains
Selkirk Mts.
Wrangell Mts.
Queen Charlotte Is.
Vancouver I.
Fairbanks
Anchorage
Whitehorse
Dawson
Juneau
Skagway
Inuvik
Yellowknife
Prince George
Edmonton
Calgary
Vancouver
Victoria
Seattle
Tacoma
Spokane
Lethbridge
Medicine Hat
Saskatoon
Regina
Moose Jaw
Prince Albert
Winnipeg
Minneapolis
Lake Winnipeg
Projection: Bonne
ALASKA
1:30 000 000
100 0 100 200 300 miles
100 0 200 400 km
RUSSIAN FED.
BERING SEA
Aleutian Is.
Brooks Range
Alaska Range
Seward Pen.
Nome
Kodiak I.
GULF OF ALASKA
Alaska Peninsula
Bristol Bay
West from Greenwich
1
2
3
10

HAWAII
1:10 000 000

Projection: Albers' Equal Area with two standard parallels

West from Greenwich

1:12 000 000

NICARAGUA

Masaya
Granada
Rama
Bluefields
Managua
L. de Nicaragua
Rivas
Jugalpa
San Juan
San Juan del Norte
S. Juan del Sur

Islas del Maíz (Nic., U.S.)
I. de San Andrés (Colombia)
Cayos de Albuquerque (Colombia)

Nicoya
Puntarenas
C.Blanco
San José
COSTA RICA
Cartago
G. de Nicoya
G. Dulce
C.Dulce
Pto. Armuelles
B. de Coronado
Volcán Barú 3374
David
PANAMA
La Chorrera
Santiago
Chitré
Pta.Mala
Pta. de Azuero
Golfo de Panamá
G. de Chiriquí
Isla Coiba

Cocos Ridge

Almirante
Bocas del Toro
Aguadulce
El Real
La Palma
Arch. de las Perlas
G. de los Mosquitos
Colón
Pto. Manzanillo

Golfo del Darién
G. de Morrosquillo
G. de Urabá
G. de Cupica

Barranquilla
Santa Marta
Ciénaga
Riohacha
Pta. Gallinas
Pen.de la Guajira
Uribia
Cartagena
Sabanalarga
Soledad
Fundación
Valledupar
Maicao
Arjona
El Carmen
Calamar
Mompós
El Banco
Sincelejo
Montería
Turbo
Riosucio
Jurado

Maracaibo
Machiques
Lago de Maracaibo
La Ceiba
El Tablazo
Cabimas
Lagunillas
San Felipe
Valencia
Sta. Carlos
Trujillo
Acarigua
Valera
Barinas
San Juan de los Morros
CARACAS
La Guaira
Puerto Cabello
Barcelona
El Tigre
Cumaná
Port of Spain
TRINIDAD & TOB.
Maturín

Curaçao (Neth.)
Aruba (Neth.)
Bonaire (Neth.)
G. de Venezuela
Pen. de Paraguaná
Coro
La Vela
Los Roques (Ven.)
La Orchila (Ven.)
I. La Tortuga (Ven.)
Margarita (Ven.)
I. Blanquilla (Ven.)
Los Hermanos (Ven.)
St. George's
GRENADA
The Grenadines
Tobago
Scarborough
Carúpano
Río Claro

VENEZUELA
San Cristóbal
Cúcuta
Rubio
Pamplona
Bucaramanga
Arauca
San Fernando de Apure
Pto. Páez
Pto. Carreño
Pto. Ayacucho
Caicara
Ciudad Bolívar
Soledad
El Tigre
Barrancas
Tumereno
El Dorado
Mt. Roraima 2810
El Callao
Guasipati
Upata

GUYANA
Kaieteur Falls
Mazaruni
Bartica
Morawhanna

COLOMBIA
Medellín
Manizales
Pereira
Cartago
Armenia
Ibagué
Buga
Cali
Palmira
BOGOTÁ
Tunja
Chiquinquirá
Girardot
Neiva
Popayán
Pasto
Tumaco
Mocoa
Florencia
San José del Guaviare
Barranca bermeja
Yarumal
Antioquia
Quibdó
Buenaventura
Vol. Puracé 4646
Huila 5790

Esmeraldas
Tulcán
Ibarra
Otavalo
Cayambe
Quito
Cotopaxi 5896
Latacunga
Ambato
Riobamba
Chimborazo 6267
Guayaquil
Milagro
Babahoyo
ECUADOR
Bahía de Caráquez
Manta
Portoviejo
Montecristi
Jipijapa
Sta. Elena
Salinas
Santa Elena
G. de Guayaquil
Cuenca
Azogues
Machala
Loja
Zaruma
Saraguro

Equator

Malpelo (Colombia)

I. Gorgona

PERU
Iquitos
Nauta
Requena
Yurimaguas
Moyobamba
Tarapoto
Chachapoyas
Cajamarca
Chiclayo
Trujillo
Chimbote
Huaraz
Huascarán 6768
Huánuco
Cerro de Pasco
LIMA
Callao
Huancayo
Huancavelica
Ayacucho
Ica
Pisco
Cuzco
Sicuani
Arequipa
Juliaca
Puno
Lago Titicaca
Moquegua
Tacna
Arica
Iquique
Pisagua

Talara
Sullana
Paita
Piura
Catacaos
Chulucanas
Desierto de Sechura
Pta.Negra
Bayovar

AMAZONAS
Manaus
Barcelos
Negro
Japurá
Solimões (Amazonas)
Tefé
São Paulo de Olivença
Humaitá
Porto Velho
RONDÔNIA
Rio Branco
Guajará-Mirim
ACRE
Cruzeiro do Sul
Tarauacá
Feijó
Sena Madureira

BOLIVIA
La Paz
Illimani 6462
Cochabamba
Oruro
Santa Cruz
Sucre
Potosí
Uyuni
Tupiza
Tarija
Villazón
Trinidad
Riberalta
Puerto Heath
Lago Poopó
Salar de Uyuni
Lago Titicaca

CHILE
Tocopilla
Calama
Pta. Angamos

ARGENTINA
PARAGUAY
Chaco Boreal

PACIFIC OCEAN

Milne Edwards Trench
Peru Trench
Chile Trench

Projection: Sanson-Flamsteed's Sinusoidal

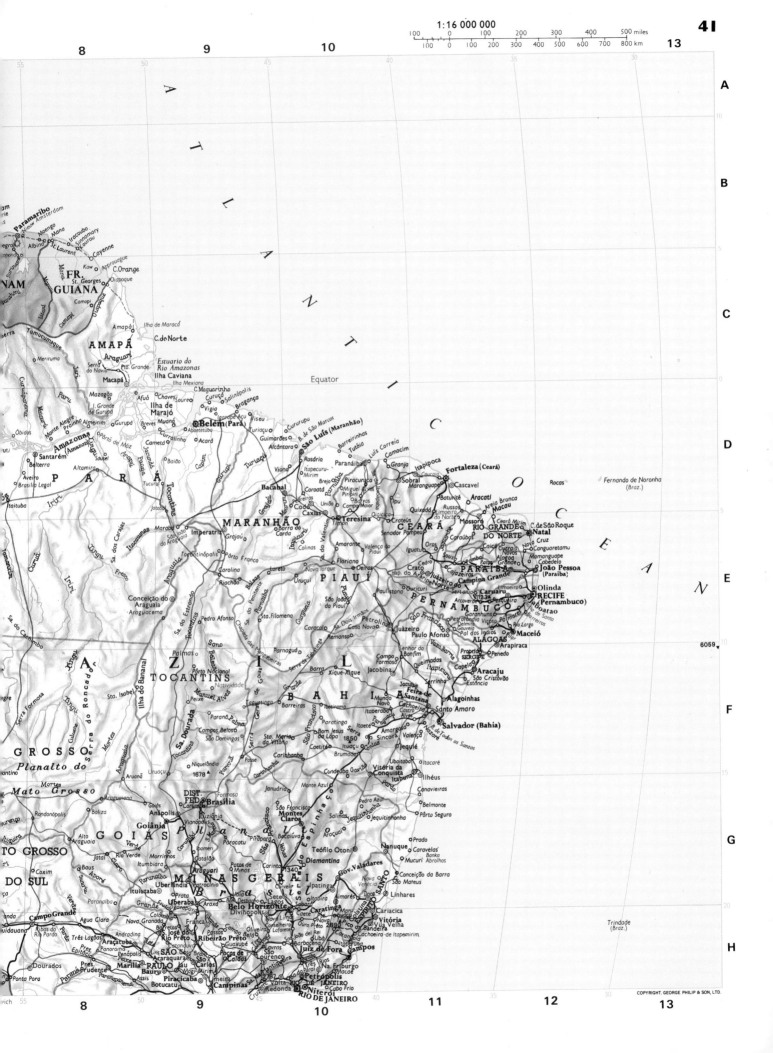

1:16 000 000

100 50 0   100   200   300 miles
100   0   100 200 300 400
km

Projection: Sanson-Flamsteed's Sinusoidal

60 West from Greenwich 55

COPYRIGHT GEORGE PHILIP & SON LTD

INDEX

he index contains the names of all the principal places and features shown on
e maps. Each name is followed by an additional entry in italics giving the
ountry or region within which it is located.

hysical features composed of a proper name (Erie) and a description (Lake)
re positioned alphabetically by the proper name. The description is positioned
fter the proper name and is usually abbreviated.

he number in bold type which follows each name in the index refers to the
umber of the map page where that feature or place will be found. This is
usually the largest scale at which the place or feature appears. The letter and
figure which are in bold type immediately after the page number give the grid
square on the map page, within which the feature is situated. The letter
represents the latitude and the figure the longitude.

In some cases the feature itself may fall within the specified square, while the
name is outside. This is usually the case only with features which are larger
than a grid square. Rivers are indexed to their mouths or confluences, and carry
the symbol ≈ after their names. A solid square ■ follows the name of a country
while, an open square □ refers to a first order administrative area.

Abbreviations used in the index:

Afghan - Afghanistan	Dom. Rep. - Dominican Republic	Mt(s). - Mount(s), Mountains(s)	S. - South
Arch. - Archipelago	Eq. - Equatorial	N. - North	S. Arabia - Saudi Arabia
Amer. - America	Fin. - Finland	N.Z. - New Zealand	Str. - Strait
Atl. - Atlantic	G. - Gulf	Neth. - Netherlands	Swed. - Sweden
B. - Bay	Ger. - Germany	Norw. - Norway	Switz. - Switzerland
Bulg. - Bulgaria	I(s). - Island(s), Isle(s)	Pac. - Pakistan	U.A.E. - United Arab Emirates
C. - Cape	Ind. - Indian	Pen. - Peninsula	U.K. - United Kingdom
Cent. - Central	Ire. - Ireland	Port. - Portugal	U.S.A. - United States of America
Chan. - Channel	L. - Lake, Loch, Lough	Rep. - Republic	W. - West
Den. - Denmark	Mong. - Mongolia	Rom. - Romania	Yug. - Yugoslavia

chen, Ger. ...16 C3
a, Nigeria ...26 G6
adan, Iran ...25 B3
ashiri, Japan ...21 F11
beville, France ...12 A4
eokuta, Nigeria ...26 G5
erdare, U.K. ...9 F4
erdeen, U.K. ...10 D6
erystwyth, U.K. ...9 E3
djan, Ivory Coast ...26 G4
ene, U.S.A. ...36 D7
uzzi, □ Italy ...14 C5
Dhabi, U.A.E. ...25 C4
pulco, Mexico ...38 D5
ra, Ghana ...26 G4
ill I., Ire. ...11 C1
ncagua, Argentina ...42 C3
e, □ Brazil ...40 E4
maoua, Massif de l', Cameroon ...28 C2
na, Turkey ...25 B2
is Abeba, Ethiopia ...28 C7
laide, Australia ...33 E6
n, Gulf of, Asia ...25 D3
atic Sea, Italy ...14 C6
ean Sea, Italy ...15 E11
hanistan, ■ Asia ...25 B5
ca ...30
dir, Morocco ...26 B3
a, India ...24 C4
ascalientes, Mexico ...38 C4
ggar, Algeria ...26 D6
nadabad, India ...24 D3
āz, Iran ...25 B3
rie, U.K. ...10 F5
cio, France ...14 D3
rshus, Norw. ...7 F11
a, Japan ...21 G11
n, U.S.A. ...37 B10
eyri, Iceland ...6 D4
dan, Yemen ...25 D3
asrah, Iraq ...25 B3
illah, Iraq ...25 B3
ufūf, S. Arabia ...25 C3
ut, Iraq ...25 B3
uwayt, Kuwait ...25 C3
adinah, S. Arabia ...25 C3
anamāh, S. Arabia ...25 C4
awsil, Iraq ...25 B3
atif, S. Arabia ...25 C3
ama, □ U.S.A. ...37 D9
ōas, □ Brazil ...41 E11
oinhas, Brazil ...41 F11
d, Fin. ...7 F16
ka, □ U.S.A. ...34 B4
Iulia, Rom. ...17 E11
cete, Spain ...13 C5
nia, ■ Europe ...15 D9
ny, U.S.A. ...37 B12
rta, □ Canada ...34 C8
g, Den. ...7 H10
querque, U.S.A. ...36 C5
bra Is., Africa ...30
rney, Channel Is. ...12 B2
rshot, U.K. ...9 F7
o = Halab, Syria ...34 C2
sándria, Italy ...14 B3
und, Norw. ...6 E9
tian Is., U.S.A. ...34 C2
andria = El Iskandarîya, Egypt ...27 B10
ton, U.K. ...8 D6
ve, □ Port. ...13 D1

Alger, Algeria ...26 A5
Algeria, ■ Africa ...26 C5
Algiers = Alger, Algeria ...26 A5
Alicante, Spain ...13 C5
Alice Springs, Australia ...32 C5
Alkmaar, Neth. ...16 B2
Allahabad, India ...24 C5
Allentown, U.S.A. ...37 B11
Alloa, U.K. ...10 E5
Alma Ata, Kazakhstan ...18 E8
Almería, Spain ...13 D4
Alps, Europe ...12 D7
Alsace, □ France ...12 B7
Altona, Ger. ...16 B4
Älvsborg, □ Swed. ...7 G12
Amagasaki, Japan ...21 B4
Amapá, □ Brazil ...41 C8
Amarillo, U.S.A. ...36 C6
Amazonas, ≈ S. Amer. ...41 D8
Amazonas, □ Brazil ...40 D5
Amiens, France ...12 B5
Ammān, Jordan ...25 B2
Amritsar, India ...24 B3
Amsterdam, Neth. ...16 B2
Amundsen Gulf, Canada ...34 A7
An Najaf, Iraq ...25 B3
Anaheim, U.S.A. ...36 D3
Anápolis, Brazil ...41 G9
Anchorage, Alaska ...34 B5
Ancohuma, Bolivia ...40 G5
Ancona, Italy ...14 C5
Andalucía, □ Spain ...13 D3
Andaman Is., India ...24 F7
Andes, Cord. de los, S. Amer. ...40 G4
Andhra Pradesh, □ India ...24 E4
Andorra, ■ Europe ...13 A6
Andria, Italy ...14 D7
Andros, Greece ...15 F11
Andros I., W. Indies ...39 C9
Angers, France ...12 C3
Anglesey, U.K. ...8 D3
Angola, ■ Africa ...29 G3
Angoulême, France ...12 D4
Angoumois, □ France ...12 D3
Anguilla, W. Indies ...38 J19
Anjou, □ France ...12 C3
Ankara, Turkey ...25 B2
Annaba, Algeria ...26 A6
Anshan, China ...22 B7
Antananarivo, Madagascar ...29 H9
Antarctica ...4 24C
Anticosti, Î. d', Canada ...35 D13
Antigua & Barbuda, ■ W. Indies ...38 K20
Antofagasta, Chile ...42 A2
Antrim, U.K. ...11 B5
Antwerpen, Belgium ...16 C2
Aomori, Japan ...21 F11
Apeldoorn, Neth. ...16 B2
Appalachian Mts., U.S.A. ...37 C10
Appennini, Italy ...14 C5
Ar Ramadi, Iraq ...25 B3
Ar Riyād, S. Arabia ...25 C3
Arabian Sea, Asia ...25 D5
Aracaju, Brazil ...41 F11
Arad, Rom. ...17 E10
Aragon, □ Spain ...13 B5
Arāk, Iran ...25 B3
Aral Sea = Aralskoye More, Asia ...18 E6
Aralskoye More, Asia ...18 E6
Arbil, Iraq ...25 B3
Arbroath, U.K. ...10 E6
Arctic Ocean ...4 12A
Ardabil, Iran ...25 B3

Ardennes, Belgium ...16 C2
Ardgour, U.K. ...10 E3
Arenal, Spain ...13 C7
Arequipa, Peru ...40 G4
Argentina, ■ S. Amer. ...42 E3
Århus, Den. ...7 H11
Arizona, □ U.S.A. ...36 D4
Arkansas, ≈ U.S.A. ...37 C7
Arkansas, □ U.S.A. ...37 D8
Arkhangelsk, Russia ...18 C5
Arklow, Ire. ...11 D5
Armagh, U.K. ...11 B5
Armenia, ■ Asia ...18 E5
Armenia, Colombia ...40 C3
Arnhem, Neth. ...16 C2
Arnhem Land, Australia ...32 A5
Arran, U.K. ...10 F3
Artois, □ France ...12 A5
Aru Is., Indonesia ...23 D5
Arunachal Pradesh, □ India ...24 C7
Asahikawa, Japan ...21 F11
Ascension, Atl. Ocean ...30 F2
Ascoli Piceno, Italy ...14 C5
Ashkhabad, Turkmenistan ...18 F6
Asmera, Ethiopia ...28 A7
Assam □ India ...24 C7
Astrakhan, Russia ...18 E5
Asturias, □ Spain ...13 A2
Asunción, Paraguay ...42 B5
Aswân, Egypt ...27 D11
Asyût, Egypt ...27 C11
Athabasca, L., Canada ...34 C9
Athens = Athínai, Greece ...15 F10
Athínai, Greece ...15 F10
Athlone, Ire. ...11 C4
Atlanta, U.S.A. ...37 D10
Atlantic Ocean ...2
Auckland, N.Z. ...31 G5
Augsburg, Ger. ...16 D5
Augusta, U.S.A. ...37 D10
Aust-Agder, □ Norw. ...7 G9
Austin, U.S.A. ...36 D7
Australia, ■ ...32
Australian Alps, Australia ...33 F8
Australian Capital Territory, □ Australia ...33 F8
Austria, ■ Europe ...16 E6
Auvergne, □ France ...12 D5
Avellaneda, Argentina ...42 C5
Aviemore, U.K. ...10 D5
Avignon, France ...12 D6
Avila, Spain ...13 B3
Avon, □ U.K. ...9 F5
Ayers Rock, Australia ...32 D5
Ayr, U.K. ...10 F4
Azerbaijan, ■ Asia ...18 E5
Azores, Atl. Ocean ...2 C8
Azovskoye More, Ukraine ...18 E4

B

Bābol, Iran ...25 B4
Bacău, Rom. ...17 E13
Bacabal, Brazil ...41 D10
Badajoz, Spain ...13 C2
Badalona, Spain ...13 B7
Baden-Württemberg, □ Ger. ...16 D4
Badenoch, U.K. ...10 E4
Baffin Bay, N. Amer. ...35 A13
Baffin I., Canada ...35 B12
Baghdād, Iraq ...25 B3
Bahamas, ■ W. Indies ...39 C9
Bahia, □ Brazil ...41 F10

Bahía Blanca, Argentina ...42 D4
Bahrain, ■ Asia ...25 C4
Baidoa, Somalia ...30 F8
Baja California, □ Mexico ...38 B2
Bakersfield, U.S.A. ...36 C3
Bakhtaran, Iran ...25 B3
Baku, Azerbaijan ...18 E5
Balboa, Panama ...38 H14
Balearas, Is., Spain ...13 C6
Bali, Indonesia ...23 D3
Balkhash, Ozero, Kazakhstan ...18 E8
Ballarat, Australia ...33 F7
Ballater, U.K. ...10 D5
Ballymena, □ U.K. ...11 B5
Ballymoney, □ U.K. ...11 A5
Balmoral, U.K. ...10 D5
Baltic Sea, Europe ...7 H15
Baltimore, U.S.A. ...37 C11
Bamako, Mali ...26 F3
Bamberg, Ger. ...16 D5
Banbridge, U.K. ...11 B5
Bandon, Ire. ...11 E3
Bandung, Indonesia ...23 D2
Banff, U.K. ...10 D6
Bangalore, India ...24 F4
Banghāzi, Libya ...27 B8
Bangkok, Thailand ...23 B2
Bangladesh, ■ Asia ...24 D6
Bangor, U.K. ...11 B6
Bangui, Cent. Afr. Rep. ...28 D3
Banjarmasin, Indonesia ...23 D3
Banks I., Canada ...34 A7
Bantry, Ire. ...11 E2
Baotou, China ...22 B5
Baranof I., Alaska ...34 C6
Barbados, ■ W. Indies ...38 P22
Barbuda, W. Indies ...38 K20
Barcelona, Spain ...13 B7
Bardsey I., U.K. ...8 E3
Bareilly, India ...24 C4
Barents Sea, Arctic ...18 B4
Bari, Italy ...14 D7
Barkly Tableland, Australia ...32 B6
Barletta, Italy ...14 D7
Barnsley, U.K. ...8 D6
Barquisimeto, Venezuela ...40 A5
Barra, U.K. ...10 E1
Barrancabermeja, Colombia ...40 B4
Barranquilla, Colombia ...40 A4
Barrow-in-Furness, U.K. ...8 C4
Barry, U.K. ...9 F4
Basel, Switz. ...16 E3
Basildon, U.K. ...9 F8
Basilicata, □ Italy ...14 D6
Basingstoke, U.K. ...9 F6
Bass Strait, Australia ...33 F8
Basse Terre, Guadeloupe ...38 L20
Bath, U.K. ...9 F5
Baton Rouge, U.S.A. ...37 D8
Bauru, Brazil ...41 H9
Bayern, □ Ger. ...16 D5
Baykal, Ozero, Russia ...19 D11
Bayonne, France ...12 E3
Bayrūt, Lebanon ...25 B2
Beaujolais, France ...12 C6
Beaumont, U.S.A. ...37 D8
Bedford, U.K. ...9 E7
Bedfordshire, □ U.K. ...9 E7
Beijing, China ...22 C6
Beira, Mozambique ...29 H7
Belcher Is., Canada ...35 C12
Belém, Brazil ...41 D9
Belet Uen, Somalia ...30 F8

Belfast, U.K. ...11 B6
Belgium, ■ Europe ...16 C2
Belgrade = Beograd, Yug. ...15 B9
Belize, ■ Cent. Amer. ...38 D7
Belmopan, Belize ...38 D7
Belo Horizonte, Brazil ...41 G10
Belorussia, ■ Europe ...18 D3
Beloye More, Russia ...18 C4
Ben Nevis, U.K. ...10 E4
Benares = Varanasi, India ...24 C5
Benbecula, U.K. ...10 D1
Bengal, B. of, Ind. Ocean ...24 E6
Bengbu, China ...22 C6
Benguela, Angola ...29 G2
Beni Suef, Egypt ...27 C11
Benidorm, Spain ...13 C5
Benin, ■ Africa ...26 G5
Benin, Bight of, Africa ...26 H5
Benin City, Nigeria ...26 G6
Benoni, S. Africa ...29 K5
Benue, ≈ Africa ...26 G6
Benxi, China ...22 B7
Beograd, Yug. ...15 B9
Bergamo, Italy ...14 B3
Bergen, Norw. ...7 F8
Bering Sea, Arctic ...19 D17
Berkeley, U.S.A. ...36 C2
Berkshire, □ U.K. ...9 F6
Berlin, Ger. ...16 B6
Bermuda, ■ Atl. Ocean ...39 A12
Bern, Switz. ...16 E3
Berwick-upon-Tweed, U.K. ...8 B6
Besançon, France ...12 C7
Béziers, France ...12 E5
Bhopal, India ...24 D4
Bhutan, ■ Asia ...24 C7
Białystok, Poland ...17 B11
Biarritz, France ...12 E3
Biel, Switz. ...16 E3
Bielefeld, Ger. ...16 B4
Bielsko-Biała, Poland ...17 D9
Bihar, □ India ...24 D6
Bijagos, Arquipélago dos, Guinea-Bissau ...26 F1
Bilbao, Spain ...13 A4
Billings, U.S.A. ...36 A5
Bioko, Eq. Guinea ...28 D1
Birkenhead, U.K. ...8 D4
Birmingham, U.K. ...9 E6
Birmingham, U.S.A. ...37 D9
Biscay, B. of, Europe ...12 D1
Bishkek, Kirghizia ...18 E8
Bishop Auckland, U.K. ...8 C6
Bitola, Macedonia ...15 D9
Biwa-Ko, Japan ...21 B5
Black Sea, Europe ...18 E4
Blackburn, U.K. ...8 D5
Blackpool, U.K. ...8 D4
Blanc, Mt., France ...12 D7
Blantyre, Malawi ...29 H7
Blaydon, U.K. ...8 C6
Bleikinge, □ Swed. ...7 H13
Bloemfontein, S. Africa ...29 K5
Blue Nile = Nîl el Azraq, ≈ Africa ...27 E11
Blyth, U.K. ...8 B6
Bobo-Dioulasso, Burkina Faso ...26 F4
Bochum, Ger. ...16 C3
Boden, Swed. ...6 D16
Bodmin Moor, U.K. ...9 G3
Boggeragh Mts., Ire. ...11 D3
Bogotá, Colombia ...40 C4
Böhmerwald, Ger. ...16 D6
Bolivia, ■ S. Amer. ...40 G5

43

Index

Bologna, *Italy* 14 B4
Bolton, *U.K.* 8 D5
Bombay, *India* 24 E3
Bonn, *Ger.* 16 C3
Boothia, Gulf of, *Canada* 35 A11
Bootle, *U.K.* 8 D4
Borås, *Swed.* 7 H12
Bordeaux, *France* 12 D3
Borders, □ *U.K.* 10 F5
Borlänge, *Swed.* 7 F13
Borneo, □ *Indonesia* 23 C3
Bornholm, *Den.* 7 J13
Bosnia-Herzegovina, ■ *Europe* ..14 B7
Bosporus, *Turkey* 25 A1
Boston, *U.S.A.* 37 B12
Boston, *U.K.* 8 E7
Bothnia, G. of, *Scandinavia* 6 E16
Botoşani, *Rom.* 17 E13
Botswana, ■ *Africa* 29 J4
Bouaké, *Ivory Coast* 26 G3
Boulogne, *France* 12 A4
Bourbonnais, □ *France* 12 C5
Bourges, *France* 12 C5
Bournemouth, *U.K.* 9 G6
Bowland, Forest of, *U.K.* 8 D5
Boyne, ≈ *Ire.* 11 C5
Brăila, *Rom.* 17 F13
Bradford, *U.K.* 8 D6
Braga, *Port.* 13 B1
Brahmaputra, ≈ *India* 24 C7
Brandenburg, *Ger.* 16 B6
Brantford, *Canada* 35 D11
Brasília, *Brazil* 41 G9
Braşov, *Rom.* 17 F12
Bratislava, *Slovak Rep.* 16 D8
Bratsk, *Russia* 19 D11
Braunschweig, *Ger.* 16 B5
Bray, *Ire.* 11 C5
Brazil, ■ *S. Amer.* 41 F8
Brazzaville, *Congo* 28 E3
Breadalbane, *U.K.* 10 E4
Brecon Beacons, *U.K.* 9 F4
Breda, *Neth.* 16 C2
Bremen, *Ger.* 16 B4
Bremerhaven, *Ger.* 16 B4
Brentwood, *U.K.* 9 F8
Bréscia, *Italy* 14 B4
Bressay, *U.K.* 10 A7
Brest, *France* 12 B1
Bretagne, □ *France* 12 B2
Bridgeport, *U.S.A.* 37 B12
Bridgetown, *Barbados* 38 P22
Bridgwater, *U.K.* 9 F4
Bridlington, *U.K.* 8 C7
Brighton, *U.K.* 9 G7
Bríndisi, *Italy* 15 D7
Brisbane, *Australia* 33 D9
Bristol, *U.K.* 9 F5
Bristol Channel, *U.K.* 9 F3
British Columbia, □ *Canada* 34 C7
Brno, *Czech Rep.* 16 D8
Broads, The, *U.K.* 8 E9
Brooks Range, *Alaska* 34 B5
Brugge, *Belgium* 16 C1
Brunei, ■ *Asia* 23 C3
Brussel, *Belgium* 16 C2
Bruxelles = Brussel, *Belgium* ..16 C2
Bucaramanga, *Colombia* 40 B4
Buchan, *U.K.* 10 D6
Bucharest = Bucureşti, *Rom.* ..17 F13
Buckinghamshire, □ *U.K.* 9 F7
Bucureşti, *Rom.* 17 F13
Budapest, *Hungary* 17 E9
Buenaventura, *Colombia* 40 C3
Buenos Aires, *Argentina* 42 C4
Buffalo, *U.S.A.* 37 B11
Buga, *Colombia* 40 C3
Bujumbura, *Burundi* 28 E5
Bukavu, *Zaïre* 28 E5
Bulawayo, *Zimbabwe* 29 J5
Bulgaria, ■ *Europe* 15 C11
Bûr Saîd, *Egypt* 27 B11
Bûr Sûdân, *Sudan* 27 E12
Burgas, *Bulg.* 15 C12
Burgenland, □ *Austria* 16 E8
Burgos, *Spain* 13 A4
Burkina Faso, ■ *Africa* 26 F4
Burma, ■ *Asia* 24 D8
Bursa, *Turkey* 25 A1
Burton-on-Trent, *U.K.* 8 E6
Buru, *Indonesia* 23 D4
Burundi, ■ *Africa* 28 E5
Buskerud, □ *Norw.* 7 F10
Bute, *U.K.* 10 F3
Bydgoszcz, *Poland* 17 B8
Bylot I., *Canada* 35 A12
Bytom, *Poland* 17 C9

C

Cabimas, *Venezuela* 40 A4
Cabinda, □ *Angola* 28 F2
Cáceres, *Spain* 13 C2
Cádiz, *Spain* 13 D2
Caen, *France* 12 B3
Caernarfon B., *U.K.* 8 D3
Cágliari, *Italy* 14 E3
Caha Mts., *Ire.* 11 E2
Cairngorm Mts., *U.K.* 10 D5

Cairo = El Qâhira, *Egypt* 27 B11
Calabar, *Nigeria* 26 G6
Calabria, □ *Italy* 14 E7
Calais, *France* 12 A4
Calcutta, *India* 24 D6
Calgary, *Canada* 34 C8
Cali, *Colombia* 40 C3
Calicut, *India* 24 F4
California, □ *U.S.A.* 36 C2
Callao, *Peru* 40 F3
Caltanissetta, *Italy* 14 F5
Camagüey, *Cuba* 39 C9
Cambodia, ■ *Asia* 23 B2
Camborne, *U.K.* 9 G2
Cambrian Mts., *U.K.* 9 E4
Cambridge, *U.K.* 9 E8
Cambridgeshire, □ *U.K.* 9 E8
Camden, *U.S.A.* 37 C12
Cameroon, ■ *Africa* 28 C2
Cameroon, Mt., *Cameroon* 28 D1
Campania, □ *Italy* 14 D6
Campbeltown, *U.K.* 10 F3
Campeche, G. de, *Mexico* 38 D6
Campina Grande, *Brazil* 41 E11
Campinas, *Brazil* 41 H9
Campo Grande, *Brazil* 41 H8
Campos, *Brazil* 41 H10
Canada, ■ *N. Amer.* 34 C10
Canarias, Is., *Atl. Ocean* 26 C1
Canaveral, C., *U.S.A.* 37 E10
Canberra, *Australia* 33 F8
Cannes, *France* 12 E7
Canouan, *W. Indies* 38 Q20
Cantabria, □ *Spain* 13 A3
Canterbury, *U.K.* 9 F9
Canton = Guangzhou, *China* ..22 D6
Cape Province, □ *S. Africa* 29 L4
Cape Town, *S. Africa* 29 L3
Cape York Pen., *Australia* 33 A7
Caprivi Strip, *Namibia* 29 H4
Caracas, *Venezuela* 40 A5
Caratinga, *Brazil* 41 G10
Cardiff, *U.K.* 9 F4
Cardigan B., *U.K.* 9 E3
Carlisle, *U.K.* 8 C5
Carlow, *Ire.* 11 D5
Carmarthen B., *U.K.* 9 F3
Carnegie, L., *Australia* 32 D3
Caroline Is., *Pac. Ocean* 3 D17
Carpathians, *Europe* 17 E12
Carpentaria, Gulf of, *Australia* ..33 A6
Carrara, *Italy* 14 B4
Carrickfergus, *U.K.* 11 B6
Cartagena, *Spain* 13 D5
Cartagena, *Colombia* 40 A3
Cartago, *Colombia* 40 C3
Caruaru, *Brazil* 41 E11
Carúpano, *Venezuela* 40 A6
Casablanca, *Morocco* 26 B3
Caspian Sea, *Asia* 18 G6
Castellón de la Plana, *Spain* ..13 C5
Castilla - La Mancha, □ *Spain* ..13 C3
Castilla y Leon, □ *Spain* 13 B3
Castries, *St. Lucia* 38 N21
Cataluña, □ *Spain* 13 B6
Catánia, *Italy* 14 F6
Catanzaro, *Italy* 14 E7
Cavan, □ *Ire.* 11 B4
Caviana, I., *Brazil* 41 C9
Ceara, □ *Brazil* 41 E11
Cebu, *Philippines* 23 B4
Cedar L., *Canada* 34 C10
Celebes Sea, *Asia* 23 C4
Celebes = Sulawesi, *Indonesia* ..23 D4
Central, □ *U.K.* 10 E4
Central African Rep., ■ *Africa* ..28 C4
Central America, *N. Amer.* 38 E7
Ceram, *Indonesia* 23 D4
Cerignola, *Italy* 14 D6
Ceylon = Sri Lanka, ■ *Asia* ..24 G5
Chad, ■ *Africa* 27 E8
Champagne, □ *France* 12 B6
Chang, ≈ *China* 22 C4
Changchun, *China* 22 B7
Changsha, *China* 22 D6
Changzhou, *China* 22 C7
Channel Is., □ *U.K.* 12 B2
Charleston, *U.S.A.* 37 D10
Charlotte, *U.S.A.* 37 C10
Charlottenburg, *Ger.* 16 B6
Charlottetown, *Canada* 35 D13
Chatham, *U.K.* 9 F8
Chattanooga, *U.S.A.* 37 C9
Cheju Do, *S. Korea* 22 C7
Chelmsford, *U.K.* 9 F8
Cheltenham, *U.K.* 9 F5
Chelyabinsk, *Russia* 18 D7
Chemnitz, *Ger.* 16 C6
Chengdu, *China* 22 C5
Cherbourg, *France* 12 B3
Cheremkhovo, *Russia* 19 D11
Chesapeake B., *U.S.A.* 37 C11
Cheshire, □ *U.K.* 8 D5
Chester, *U.K.* 8 D5
Chesterfield, *U.K.* 8 D6
Cheviot Hills, *U.K.* 8 B5
Chiba, *Japan* 21 B7
Chicago, *U.S.A.* 37 B9
Chichagof I., *Alaska* 34 C6

Chiclayo, *Peru* 40 E3
Chihuahua, *Mexico* 38 B3
Chile, ■ *S. Amer.* 42 D2
Chiloé I. de, *Chile* 42 E2
Chiltern Hills, *U.K.* 9 F7
Chimborazo, *Ecuador* 40 D3
China, ■ *Asia* 22 C4
Chingola, *Zambia* 29 G5
Chişinau = Kishinev, *Moldavia* ..18 E3
Chita, *Russia* 19 D12
Chittagong, *Bangladesh* 24 D7
Chongqing, *China* 22 D5
Chonos, Arch. de los, *Chile* ..42 E2
Chorzów, *Poland* 17 C9
Christchurch, *N.Z.* 31 K4
Christmas I., *Australia* 23 E2
Chukotskoye More, *Russia* ..19 C19
Chungking = Chongqing, *China* ..22 D5
Ciénaga, *Colombia* 40 A4
Cienfuegos, *Cuba* 39 C8
Cincinnati, *U.S.A.* 37 C10
Ciudad Bolivar, *Venezuela* 40 B6
Ciudad Guayana, *Venezuela* ..40 B6
Ciudad Juárez, *Mexico* 38 A3
Ciudad Real, *Spain* 13 C4
Clacton, *U.K.* 9 F9
Clare, □ *Ire.* 11 D2
Cleethorpes, *U.K.* 8 D7
Clermont-Ferrand, *France* 12 D5
Cleveland, *U.S.A.* 37 B10
Cleveland, □ *U.K.* 8 C6
Clonmel, *Ire.* 11 D4
Cluj-Napoca, *Rom.* 17 E11
Clwyd, □ *U.K.* 8 D4
Clyde, ≈ *U.K.* 10 F5
Clyde, Firth of, *U.K.* 10 F3
Clydebank, *U.K.* 10 F4
Coalville, *U.K.* 8 E6
Coast Ranges, *U.S.A.* 36 C2
Coatbridge, *U.K.* 10 F4
Coats I., *Canada* 35 B11
Cobh, *Ire.* 11 E3
Cochabamba, *Bolivia* 40 G5
Cocos or Keeling Is., *Australia* ..23 E1
Coimbra, *Port.* 13 B1
Colchester, *U.K.* 9 F8
Coleraine, □ *U.K.* 11 A5
Coll, *U.K.* 10 E2
Cologne = Köln, *Ger.* 16 C3
Colombia, ■ *S. Amer.* 40 C4
Colombo, *Sri Lanka* 24 G5
Colón, *Panama* 38 H14
Colonsay, *U.K.* 10 E2
Colorado, □ *U.S.A.* 36 C5
Colorado, ≈ *U.S.A.* 36 D4
Colorado Springs, *U.S.A.* 36 C6
Columbia, ≈ *U.S.A.* 36 A2
Columbia, *U.S.A.* 37 D10
Columbus, Georgia, *U.S.A.* ..37 D10
Columbus, Ohio, *U.S.A.* 37 C10
Colwyn Bay, *U.K.* 8 D4
Comeragh Mts., *Ire.* 11 D4
Como, *Italy* 14 B3
Comoros, ■ *Africa* 30 G8
Conakry, *Guinea* 26 G2
Concepcion, *Chile* 42 D2
Congo, ≈ *Africa* 28 E3
Congo, ■ *Africa* 28 E3
Congo = Zaïre, ≈ *Africa* 28 D4
Connacht, *Ire.* 11 C2
Connecticut, □ *U.S.A.* 37 B12
Connemara, *Ire.* 11 C2
Constanţa, *Rom.* 17 F14
Constantine, *Algeria* 26 A6
Cookstown, *U.K.* 11 B5
Cooper Creek, ≈ *Australia* 33 D6
Copenhagen = København, *Den.* ..7 J12
Córdoba, *Spain* 13 D3
Córdoba, *Argentina* 42 C4
Corfu = Kérkira, *Greece* 15 E8
Cork, *Ire.* 11 E3
Cornwall, □ *U.K.* 9 G3
Coronation Gulf, *Canada* 34 B8
Corpus Christi, *U.S.A.* 36 E7
Corse, *France* 14 C3
Corsica = Corse, *France* 14 C3
Corumba, *Brazil* 40 G7
Cosenza, *Italy* 14 E7
Costa Blanca, *Spain* 13 C5
Costa Brava, *Spain* 13 B7
Costa del Sol, *Spain* 13 D4
Costa Dorada, *Spain* 13 B7
Costa Rica, ■ *Cent. Amer.* 39 F8
Cote d'Ivoire = Ivory Coast,
 ■ *Africa* 26 G3
Cotonou, *Benin* 26 G5
Cotopaxi, *Ecuador* 40 D3
Cotswold Hills, *U.K.* 9 F6
Cottbus, *Ger.* 16 C7
Coventry, *U.K.* 9 E6
Craiova, *Rom.* 17 F11
Cremona, *Italy* 14 B4
Crete = Kriti, *Greece* 15 G11
Crewe, *U.K.* 8 D5
Croatia, ■ *Europe* 14 B6
Cuba, ■ *W. Indies* 39 C8
Cúcuta, *Colombia* 40 B4
Cuenca, *Ecuador* 40 D3

Cuenca, *Spain* 13 B4
Cuiaba, *Brazil* 41 G7
Cumaná, *Venezuela* 40 A6
Cumbernauld, *U.K.* 10 F4
Cumbria, □ *U.K.* 8 C5
Cumbrian Mts., *U.K.* 8 C4
Curaçao, *Neth. Ant.* 40 A5
Curitiba, *Brazil* 42 B7
Cuzco, *Peru* 40 F4
Cwmbran, *U.K.* 9 F4
Cyclades = Kikládhes, *Greece* ..15 F11
Cyprus, ■ *Asia* 25 B2
Czech Rep., ■ *Europe* 16 D7
Czestochowa, *Poland* 17 C9

D

Dakar, *Senegal* 26 F1
Dalian, *China* 22 C7
Dallas, *U.S.A.* 37 D7
Damaraland, *Namibia* 29 J3
Damascus = Dimashq, *Syria* ..25 B2
Dandong, *China* 22 B7
Danube = Dunarea, ≈ *Europe* ..17 F14
Dar-es-Salaam, *Tanzania* 28 F7
Dardanelles, *Turkey* 25 A1
Darién, G. del, *S. Amer.* 40 B3
Darling, ≈ *Australia* 33 E7
Darlington, *U.K.* 8 C6
Darmstadt, *Ger.* 16 D4
Dartmoor, *U.K.* 9 G4
Dartmouth, *Canada* 35 D13
Darwin, *Australia* 32 A5
Datong, *China* 22 B6
Dauphine, □ *France* 12 D6
Davao, *Philippines* 23 C4
Davis Str., *N. Amer.* 35 B14
Dayton, *U.S.A.* 37 C10
Dead Sea, *Asia* 25 B2
Deal, *U.K.* 9 F9
Dean, Forest of, *U.K.* 9 F5
Debrecen, *Hungary* 17 E10
Delaware, □ *U.S.A.* 37 C11
Delhi, *India* 24 C4
Denmark, ■ *Europe* 7 J10
Denver, *U.S.A.* 36 C6
Derby, *U.K.* 8 E6
Derbyshire, □ *U.K.* 8 D6
Derryveagh Mts., *Ire.* 11 A4
Des Moines, *U.S.A.* 37 B8
Dessau, *Ger.* 16 C6
Detroit, *U.S.A.* 37 B10
Devon, □ *U.K.* 9 G4
Devon I., *Canada* 35 A11
Dezfûl, *Iran* 25 B3
Dhaka, *Bangladesh* 24 D7
Dhodhekanisos, *Greece* 15 F12
Dieppe, *France* 12 B4
Dijon, *France* 12 C6
Dimashq, *Syria* 25 B2
Dingle B., *Ire.* 11 D1
Dingwall, *U.K.* 10 D4
Disappointment, L., *Australia* ..32 C3
Diyarbakir, *Turkey* 25 B3
Djibouti, ■ *Africa* 30 D8
Dneropetrovsk, *Ukraine* 18 E4
Dnepropetrovsk, *Ukraine* 18 E4
Dhaka, *Bangladesh* 24 D7
Dodecanese = Dodekanisos,
Dolomiti, *Italy* 14 A4
Dominica, ■ *W. Indies* 38 M20
Dominican Rep., ■ *W. Indies* ..39 D10
Don, ≈ *Russia* 18 E5
Doncaster, *U.K.* 8 D6
Donegal, *Ire.* 11 B3
Donetsk, *Ukraine* 18 E4
Dordrecht, *Neth.* 16 C2
Dornoch, *U.K.* 10 D4
Dorset, □ *U.K.* 9 G5
Dortmund, *Ger.* 16 C3
Douala, *Cameroon* 28 D1
Douglas, *U.K.* 8 C3
Dounreay, *U.K.* 10 C5
Douro, ≈ *Port.* 13 B1
Dover, *U.K.* 9 F9
Down, □ *U.K.* 11 B6
Drakensberg, *S. Africa* 29 K5
Drammen, *Norw.* 7 G11
Dresden, *Ger.* 16 C6
Drogheda, *Ire.* 11 C5
Dublin, *Ire.* 11 C5
Dubrovnik, *Croatia* 15 C8
Dudley, *U.K.* 9 E5
Duisburg, *Ger.* 16 C3
Duluth, *U.S.A.* 37 A8
Dumbarton, *U.K.* 10 F4
Dumfries, *U.K.* 10 F5
Dumfries and Galloway, □ *U.K.* ..10 F5
Dumyât, *Egypt* 27 B11
Dun Laoghaire, *Ire.* 11 C5
Dunarea, ≈ *Europe* 17 F14
Dundalk, *Ire.* 11 B5
Dundee, *U.K.* 10 E5
Dunedin, *N.Z.* 31 L3
Dunfermline, *U.K.* 10 E5
Dungannon, *U.K.* 11 B5
Dungarvan, *Ire.* 11 D4
Dunkerque, *France* 12 A5
Durango, *Mexico* 38 C4
Durban, *S. Africa* 29 K6
Durham, □ *U.K.* 8 C6
Dushanbe, *Tajikistan* 18 F7

Düsseldorf, *Ger.* 16
Dyfed, □ *U.K.* 9

E

East China Sea, *Asia* 22
East Kilbride, *U.K.* 10
East London, *S. Africa* 29
East Siberian Sea, *Arctic* ....19 B
East Sussex, □ *U.K.* 9
Eastbourne, *U.K.* 9
Easter Is., *Pac. Ocean* 2
Ebbw Vale, *U.K.* 9
Ebro, ≈ *Spain* 13
Ech Cheliff, *Algeria* 26
Ecuador, ■ *S. Amer.* 40
Eday, *U.K.* 10
Edinburgh, *U.K.* 10
Edmonton, *Canada* 34
Edward, L., *Africa* 28
Egypt, ■ *Africa* ....27 C
Eifel, *Ger.* 16
Eigg, *U.K.* 10
Eighty Mile Beach, *Australia* 32
Eindhoven, *Neth.* 16
El Faiyûm, *Egypt* ....27 C
El Ferrol, *Spain* 13
El Gîza, *Egypt* ....27 C
El Iskandarîya, *Egypt* ....27 B
El Khartûm, *Sudan* ....27 E
El Mahalla el Kubra, *Egypt* ..27 B
El Mansûra, *Egypt* ....27 B
El Minyâ, *Egypt* ....27 C
El Obeid, *Sudan* ....27 E
El Paso, *U.S.A.* 36
El Qâhira, *Egypt* ....27 B
El Salvador, ■ *Cent. Amer.* 38
El Suweis, *Egypt* ....27 C
Elba, *Italy* 14
Elbe, ≈ *Ger.* 16
Elblag, *Poland* 17
Elburz Mts., *Iran* 25
Elche, *Spain* 13
Eleuthera I., *W. Indies* 39
Elgin, *U.K.* 10
Ellesmere Port, *U.K.* 8
Emilia Romagna, □ *Italy* 14
England, □ *U.K.* 9
English Channel, *Europe* 9
Ennis, *Ire.* 11
Enniscorthy, *Ire.* 11
Enschede, *Neth.* 16
Enugu, *Nigeria* 26
Equatorial Guinea, ■ *Africa* 28
Erawadi Myit, ≈ *Burma* 24
Erfurt, *Ger.* 16
Erie, L., *N. Amer.* ....35 C
Eritrea, ■ *Africa* 25
Erzurum, *Turkey* 25
Esbjerg, *Den.* 7
Esfahân, *Iran* 25
Eskilstuna, *Swed.* ....7 C
Eskisehir, *Turkey* 25
Espirito Santo, □ *Brazil* ....41 C
Essen, *Ger.* 16
Essex, □ *U.K.* 9
Estonia, ■ *Europe* 18
Ethiopia, ■ *Africa* 28
Etna, Mt., *Italy* 14
Euphrates, ≈ *Asia* 25
Evansville, *U.S.A.* 37
Everest, Mt., *Nepal* 24
Everglades, *U.S.A.* 37
Évora, *Port.* 13
Évvoia, *Greece* 15
Exeter, *U.K.* 9
Exmoor, *U.K.* 9
Extremadura, □ *Spain* 13
Eyre, L., *Australia* 33
Eyre Peninsula, *Australia* 32

F

Fairbanks, *Alaska* 34
Falkirk, *U.K.* 10
Falkland Is., *Atl. Ocean* 42
Fareham, *U.K.* 9
Farnborough, *U.K.* 9
Faroe Is., *Atl. Ocean* 5
Feira de Santana, *Brazil* 41
Fens, The, *U.K.* 8
Fermanagh, □ *U.K.* 11
Ferrara, *Italy* 14
Fès, *Morocco* 26
Fetlar, *U.K.* 10
Fife, □ *U.K.* 10
Fiji, ■ *Pac. Ocean* 31
Finland, ■ *Europe* 6
Finnmark, □ *Norw.* 6
Firenze, *Italy* 14
Flandre, *Belgium* 16
Fleetwood, *U.K.* 8
Flensburg, *Ger.* 16
Flinders I., *Australia* 33
Flint, *U.S.A.* 37
Florence = Firenze, *Italy* 14
Flores, *Indonesia* 23
Florida, □ *U.S.A.* 37
Fóggia, *Italy* 14

Index

kestone, *U.K.* 9 F9
de France, *Martinique* 38 N20
Smith, *U.S.A.* 37 C8
Wayne, *U.S.A.* 37 B9
William, *U.K.* 10 E3
Worth, *U.S.A.* 36 D7
taleza, *Brazil* 41 D11
th, Firth of, *U.K.* 10 E6
la, *U.K.* 10 A6
Channel, *Canada* 35 B11
nce, ■ *Europe* 12 C4
nche-Comte, □ *France* 12 C6
nkfurt am Main, *Ger.* 16 C4
an der Oder, *Ger.* 16 B7
nkische Alb, *Ger.* 16 D5
ser I., *Australia* 33 D9
serburgh, *U.K.* 10 D6
deriskavn, *Den.* 7 H11
derikstad, *Norw.* 7 G11
etown, *Sierra Leone* 26 G2
iburg, *Ger.* 16 D3
nch Guiana, ■ *S. Amer.* 41 C8
sno, *U.S.A.* 36 C3
li Venezia Giulia, □ *Italy* 14 A5
n, L., *Australia* 33 E6
nze = Bishkek, *Kirghizia* 18 E8
i-San, *Japan* 21 B6
kuoka, *Japan* 21 C2
kushima, *Japan* 21 G11
nabashi, *Japan* 21 B7
neaux Group, *Australia* 33 G8
th, *Ger.* 16 D5
shun, *China* 22 B6
zhou, *China* 22 D6
n, *Den.* 7 J11

bon, ■ *Africa* 28 E2
borone, *Botswana* 29 J5
irdner, L., *Australia* 32 E6
lati, *Rom.* 17 F14
lapagos Is., *Pac. Ocean* 2 E5
lashiels, *U.K.* 10 F6
licia, □ *Spain* 13 A1
llivare, *Swed.* 6 C16
lloway, *U.K.* 10 G4
lveston, *U.S.A.* 37 E8
lway, *Ire.* 11 C2
mbia, ■ *Africa* 26 F1
mboa, *Panama* 38 H14
nga, ≈ *Ind./Bangla.* 24 C4
nges = Ganga, ≈ *Ind./Bangla.* 24 C4
oxiong, *Taiwan* 22 D7
rda, L. di, *Italy* 14 B4
ry, *U.S.A.* 37 B9
scogne, □ *France* 12 E3
spé, Pén. de, *Canada* 35 D13
teshead, *U.K.* 8 C6
tun, *Panama* 38 H14
vle, *Swed.* 7 F14
vleborg, □ *Swed.* 7 F14
za, *Israel* 25 B2
ziantep, *Turkey* 25 B2
dansk, *Poland* 17 A9
nynia, *Poland* 17 A9
elong, *Australia* 33 F7
elsenkirchen, *Ger.* 16 C3
nève, *Switz.* 16 E3
nova, *Italy* 14 B3
nt, *Belgium* 16 C1
orge Town, *Malaysia* 23 C2
orgetown, *Guyana* 40 B7
orgia, ■ *Asia* 18 E5
orgia, □ *U.S.A.* 37 D10
era, *Ger.* 16 C6
rmany, ■ *Europe* 16 C5
rmiston, *S. Africa* 29 K5
rona, *Spain* 13 B7
hana, ■ *Africa* 26 G4
ant's Causeway, *U.K.* 11 A5
braltar, □ *U.K.* 13 D3
bson Desert, *Australia* 32 C3
fu, *Japan* 21 B5
gha, *U.K.* 10 F3
jón, *Spain* 13 A3
llingham, *U.K.* 9 F8
sborne, *N.Z.* 31 H7
øvik, *Norw.* 7 F11
asgow, *U.K.* 10 F4
endale, *U.S.A.* 36 D3
enrothes, *U.K.* 10 E5
iwice, *Poland* 17 C9
ogów, *Poland* 16 C8
oucester, *U.K.* 9 F5
oucestershire, □ *U.K.* 9 F5
oa, □ *India* 24 E3
iânia, *Brazil* 41 G9
iás, *Brazil* 41 F9
ood Hope, C. of, *S. Africa* 29 L3
orkiy = Nizhniy Novgorod, *Russia* .18 D5
örlitz, *Ger.* 16 C7
osport, *U.K.* 9 G6
iteborg, *Swed.* 7 H11
otland, *Swed.* 7 H15
italand, *Swed.* 7 G12
zo, *Malta* 14 F6
mpian, □ *U.K.* 10 D6
mpian Highlands, *U.K.* 10 E4

Gran Canaria, *Canary Is.* 26 C1
Granada, *Spain* 13 D4
Grand Bahama I., *W. Indies* 39 B9
Grand Canyon, *U.S.A.* 36 C4
Grand Cayman, *W. Indies* 39 D8
Grand Rapids, *U.S.A.* 37 B9
Grangemouth, *U.K.* 10 E5
Grantham, *U.K.* 8 E7
Graz, *Austria* 16 E8
Great Abaco I., *W. Indies* 39 B9
Great Australian Bight, *Australia* 32 E4
Great Barrier Reef, *Australia* 33 B8
Great Bear L., *Canada* 34 B7
Great Divide, *Australia* 33 C8
Great Falls, *U.S.A.* 36 A4
Great Inagua I., *W. Indies* 39 C10
Great Salt Lake, *U.S.A.* 36 B4
Great Sandy Desert, *Australia* 32 C3
Great Slave L., *Canada* 34 B8
Great Victoria Desert, *Australia* 32 D4
Great Wall, The, *China* 22 C5
Great Yarmouth, *U.K.* 8 E9
Greater Antilles, *W. Indies* 39 D9
Greater Manchester, □ *U.K.* 8 D5
Greece, ■ *Europe* 15 E9
Green Bay, *U.S.A.* 37 B9
Greenland, ■ *N. Amer.* 4 A9
Greenock, *U.K.* 10 F4
Greensboro, *U.S.A.* 37 C11
Grenada, ■ *W. Indies* 38 Q20
Grenoble, *France* 12 D6
Gretna Green, *U.K.* 10 F5
Grey Range, *Australia* 33 D7
Grimsby, *U.K.* 8 D7
Groningen, *Neth.* 16 B3
Groot Karoo, *S. Africa* 29 L4
Groote Eylandt, *Australia* 33 A6
Gross Glockner, *Austria* 16 E6
Grudziadz, *Poland* 17 B9
Guadalajara, *Mexico* 38 C4
Guadalajara, *Spain* 13 B4
Guadarrama, Sierra de, *Spain* 13 B4
Guadeloupe, ■ *W. Indies* 38 L20
Guadiana, ≈ *Port.* 13 D2
Guadix, *Spain* 13 D4
Guangzhou, *China* 22 D6
Guantanamo, *Cuba* 39 C9
Guatemala, ■ *Cent. Amer.* 38 D6
Guatemala City, *Guatemala* 38 E6
Guayaquil, *Ecuador* 40 D2
Guelph, *Canada* 35 D11
Guernsey, *Channel Is.* 12 B2
Guildford, *U.K.* 9 F7
Guinea, ■ *Africa* 26 F2
Guinea-Bissau, ■ *Africa* 26 F1
Guiyang, *China* 22 D5
Gujarat, □ *India* 24 D3
Gulf, The, *Asia* 25 C4
Guyana, ■ *S. Amer.* 40 B7
Guyenne, □ *France* 12 D4
Gwalior, *India* 24 C4
Gwent, □ *U.K.* 9 F4
Gwynedd, □ *U.K.* 8 E4
Györ, *Hungary* 17 E8

Haarlem, *Neth.* 16 B2
Hachinohe, *Japan* 21 F11
Hadrian's Wall, *U.K.* 8 C5
Hagen, *Ger.* 16 C3
Haifa, *Israel* 25 B2
Hainan Dao, *China* 22 E6
Haiti, ■ *W. Indies* 39 D10
Hakodate, *Japan* 21 F11
Halab, *Syria* 25 B2
Halberstadt, *Ger.* 16 C5
Halifax, *Canada* 35 D13
Halifax, *U.K.* 8 D6
Halland, □ *Swed.* 7 H12
Halle, *Ger.* 16 C5
Halmstad, *Swed.* 7 H12
Hamā, *Syria* 25 B2
Hamadān, *Iran* 25 B3
Hamamatsu, *Japan* 21 B5
Hamar, *Norw.* 7 F11
Hamburg, *Ger.* 16 B5
Hame, □ *Fin.* 7 F17
Hameln, *Ger.* 16 B4
Hamilton, *N.Z.* 31 G5
Hamilton, *U.K.* 10 F4
Hamilton, *Canada* 35 D11
Hamm, *Ger.* 16 C3
Hammerfest, *Norw.* 6 A17
Hammond, *U.S.A.* 37 B9
Hampshire, □ *U.K.* 9 F6
Hangzhou, *China* 22 C6
Hanoi, *Vietnam* 23 A2
Hannover, *Ger.* 16 B4
Harare, *Zimbabwe* 29 H6
Harbin, *China* 22 B7
Hargeisa, *Somalia* 30 F8
Harlow, *U.K.* 9 F8
Härnösand, *Swed.* 6 E15
Harrogate, *U.K.* 8 D6
Hartlepool, *U.K.* 8 C6
Haryana, □ *India* 24 C4
Hastings, *N.Z.* 31 H6

Hastings, *U.K.* 9 G8
Haugesund, *Norw.* 7 G8
Haut Atlas, *Morocco* 26 B4
Havana = La Habana, *Cuba* 39 C8
Havant, *U.K.* 9 G7
Hawaii, *Pac. Ocean* 2
Hawaii, □ *U.S.A.* 36 H16
Hawick, *U.K.* 10 F6
Hedmark, □ *Norw.* 7 F11
Hefei, *China* 22 C6
Heidelberg, *Ger.* 16 D4
Heilbronn, *Ger.* 16 D4
Helmsdale, *U.K.* 10 C5
Helsingborg, *Swed.* 7 H12
Helsingor, *Den.* 7 H12
Helsinki, *Fin.* 7 F18
Hemel Hempstead, *U.K.* 9 F7
Hengyang, *China* 22 D6
Herat, *Afghan.* 25 B5
Hereford, *U.K.* 9 E5
Hereford & Worcester, □ *U.K.* 9 E5
Herford, *Ger.* 16 B4
Hermosillo, *Mexico* 38 B2
Hertfordshire, □ *U.K.* 9 F7
Hessen, □ *Ger.* 16 C4
Higashiōsaka, *Japan* 21 B4
High Wycombe, *U.K.* 9 F7
Highland, □ *U.K.* 10 D4
Hildesheim, *Ger.* 16 B4
Hilversum, *Neth.* 16 B3
Himachal Pradesh, □ *India* 24 C4
Himalaya, *Asia* 24 C5
Himeji, *Japan* 21 B4
Hims, *Syria* 25 B2
Hindu Kush, *Afghan.* 24 B3
Hirosaki, *Japan* 21 F11
Hiroshima, *Japan* 21 B3
Hobart, *Australia* 33 G8
Hohhot, *China* 22 B6
Hokkaido, *Japan* 21 F11
Holderness, *U.K.* 8 D7
Holguin, *Cuba* 39 C9
Hollywood, *U.S.A.* 36 D3
Honduras, ■ *Cent. Amer.* 38 E7
Hønefoss, *Norw.* 7 F11
Hong Kong, ■ *Asia* 22 D6
Honolulu, *Hawaii* 36 H16
Honshu, *Japan* 21 B4
Hordaland, □ *Norw.* 7 F9
Horn, C. = Hornos, C. de, *Chile* 42 H3
Hornos, C. de, *Chile* 42 H3
Horsens, *Den.* 7 J10
Hospitalet, *Spain* 13 B7
Houghton-le-Spring, *U.K.* 8 C6
Houston, *U.S.A.* 37 E8
Howrah, *India* 24 D6
Hoy, *U.K.* 10 C5
Hradec Kralove, *Czech Rep.* 16 C7
Huainan, *China* 22 C6
Huang, ≈ *China* 22 C6
Huascarán, *Peru* 40 E3
Huddersfield, *U.K.* 8 D6
Hudson Bay, *Canada* 35 B11
Hudson Str., *Canada* 35 B12
Huelva, *Spain* 13 D2
Huesca, *Spain* 13 A5
Hull, *U.K.* 8 D7
Humber, ≈ *U.K.* 8 D7
Humberside, □ *U.K.* 8 D7
Hungary, ■ *Europe* 17 E9
Hunsrück, *Ger.* 16 D3
Huron, L., *N. Amer.* 37 B10
Hyderabad, *India* 24 E4
Hyderabad, *Pak.* 24 C2

Iasi, *Rom.* 17 E13
Ibadan, *Nigeria* 26 G5
Ibagué, *Colombia* 40 C3
Ibiza, *Spain* 13 C6
Iceland, ■ *Europe* 6
Ichinomiya, *Japan* 21 B5
Idaho, □ *U.S.A.* 36 B3
Ikaría, *Greece* 15 F12
Île-de-France, □ *France* 12 B5
Illinois, □ *U.S.A.* 37 B9
Ilorin, *Nigeria* 26 G5
Imphal, *India* 24 D7
Inch'on, *S. Korea* 22 C7
India, ■ *Asia* 24 D4
Indian Ocean, ...24 H3
Indiana, □ *U.S.A.* 37 C9
Indianapolis, *U.S.A.* 37 C9
Indonesia, ■ *Asia* 23 D3
Indore, *India* 24 D4
Indus, ≈ *Pakistan* 24 C2
Ingolstadt, *Ger.* 16 D5
Inishowen Pen., *Ire.* 11 A4
Inner Hebrides, *U.K.* 10 E2
Innsbruck, *Austria* 16 E5
Inveraray, *U.K.* 10 E3
Invercargill, *N.Z.* 31 M2
Invergordon, *U.K.* 10 D4
Inverness, *U.K.* 10 D4
Iona, *U.K.* 10 E2
Ionian Sea, *Europe* 15 E8
Iónioi Nisoi, □ *Greece* 15 E8

Iowa, □ *U.S.A.* 37 B8
Ípiros, □ *Greece* 15 E9
Ipswich, *U.K.* 9 E9
Iquique, *Chile* 40 H4
Iquitos, *Peru* 40 D4
Iráklion, *Greece* 15 G11
Iran, ■ *Asia* 25 B4
Iraq, ■ *Asia* 25 B3
Ireland, ■ *Europe* 11 C4
Irian Jaya, □ *Indonesia* 23 D5
Irish Sea, *Europe* 8 D2
Irkutsk, *Russia* 19 D11
Irrawady = Erawadi Myit, ≈ *Burma* .24 E8
Irvine, *U.K.* 10 F4
Islay, *U.K.* 10 F2
Israel, ■ *Asia* 25 B2
Istanbul, *Turkey* 25 A1
Italy, ■ *Europe* 14 C4
Ivory Coast, ■ *Africa* 26 G3
Iwaki, *Japan* 21 G11
Iwo, *Nigeria* 26 G5
Izmir, *Turkey* 25 B1

J

Jabalpur, *India* 24 D5
Jackson, *U.S.A.* 37 D8
Jacksonville, *U.S.A.* 37 D10
Jaén, *Spain* 13 D4
Jaipur, *India* 24 C4
Jakarta, *Indonesia* 23 D2
Jamaica, ■ *W. Indies* 39 D9
James Bay, *Canada* 35 C11
Jammu & Kashmir, □ *India* 24 B3
Jämtland, □ *Norw.* 6 E13
Japan, ■ *Asia* 21 G10
Japan, Sea of, *Asia* 21 A3
Java, *Indonesia* 23 D2
Jena, *Ger.* 16 C5
Jerez, *Spain* 13 D2
Jersey, *Channel Is.* 12 B2
Jersey City, *U.S.A.* 37 B12
Jerusalem, *Israel* 25 B2
Jiddah, *S. Arabia* 25 C2
Jilin, *China* 22 B7
Jilong, *Taiwan* 22 D7
Jinan, *China* 22 C6
Jinzhou, *China* 22 B7
João Pessoa, *Brazil* 41 E12
Johannesburg, *S. Africa* 29 K5
John O'Groats, *U.K.* 10 C5
Johnstone, *U.K.* 10 F4
Jönköping, □ *Swed.* 7 H12
Jordan, ■ *Asia* 25 B2
Juàzeiro do Norte, *Brazil* 41 E11
Juiz de Fora, *Brazil* 41 H10
Jundiaí, *Brazil* 42 A7
Jura, *Europe* 12 C6
Jura, *U.K.* 10 F3

K

Kabul, *Afghan.* 25 B5
Kaduna, *Nigeria* 26 F6
Kagoshima, *Japan* 21 D2
Kaiserslautern, *Ger.* 16 D3
Kalahari, *Africa* 29 J4
Kaliningrad, *Russia* 18 D3
Kalisz, *Poland* 17 C9
Kalmar, *Swed.* 7 H14
Kamaishi, *Japan* 21 G11
Kampala, *Uganda* 28 D6
Kampuchea = Cambodia, ■ *Asia* .23 B2
Kananga, *Zaïre* 28 F4
Kanazawa, *Japan* 21 A5
Kandahar, *Afghan.* 25 B5
Kangaroo I., *Australia* 33 F6
Kano, *Nigeria* 26 F6
Kanpur, *India* 24 C5
Kansas, □ *U.S.A.* 36 C7
Kansas City, *U.S.A.* 37 C8
Kaokoveld, *Namibia* 29 H2
Kaolack, *Senegal* 26 F1
Kara Sea, *Arctic* 18 B7
Karachi, *Pak.* 24 D2
Karaganda, *Kazakhstan* 18 E8
Karbalā, *Iraq* 25 B3
Kariba L., *Africa* 29 H5
Karlskrona, *Swed.* 7 H13
Karlsruhe, *Ger.* 16 D4
Karlstad, *Swed.* 7 G12
Kärnten, □ *Austria* 16 E6
Kárpathos, *Greece* 15 G12
Kāshān, *Iran* 25 B4
Kassel, *Ger.* 16 C4
Katmandu, *Nepal* 24 C6
Katowice, *Poland* 17 C9
Katsina, *Nigeria* 26 F6
Kattegat, *Scandinavia* 7 H11
Kawaguchi, *Japan* 21 B6
Kawasaki, *Japan* 21 B6
Kayseri, *Turkey* 25 B2
Kazakhstan, ■ *Asia* 18 E7
Kazan, *Russia* 18 D5
Kecskemét, *Hungary* 17 E9
Kefallinia, *Greece* 15
Keflavik, *Iceland* 6
Keighley, *U.K.* 8 D6
Kemān, *Iran* 25 B4

Kemi, *Fin.* 6 D18
Kenitra, *Morocco* 26 B3
Kent, □ *U.K.* 9 F8
Kentucky, □ *U.S.A.* 37 C9
Kenya, ■ *Africa* 28 D7
Kenya, Mt., *Kenya* 28 E7
Kerala, □ *India* 24 F4
Kérkira, *Greece* 15 E8
Kerry, □ *Ire.* 11 D2
Keski-Suomen, □ *Fin.* 6 E18
Key West, *U.S.A.* 37 F10
Khabarovsk, *Russia* 19 E14
Kharkov, *Ukraine* 18 E4
Khartoum = El Khartūm, *Sudan* 27 E11
Khios, *Greece* 15 E11
Khulna, *Bangladesh* 24 D6
Kidderminster, *U.K.* 9 E5
Kiel, *Ger.* 16 A5
Kielce, *Poland* 17 C10
Kikládhes, *Greece* 15 F11
Kikwit, *Zaïre* 28 E3
Kildare, □ *Ire.* 11 C5
Kilimanjaro, *Tanzania* 28 E7
Kilkenny, *Ire.* 11 D4
Killarney, *Ire.* 11 D2
Kilmarnock, *U.K.* 10 F4
Kimberley, *Australia* 32 B4
Kimberley, *S. Africa* 29 K4
King I., *Australia* 33 F7
King William I., *Canada* 34 B10
Kings Lynn, *U.K.* 8 E8
Kingston, *Jamaica* 38 J17
Kingston, *U.K.* 9 F7
Kingussie, *U.K.* 10 D4
Kinshasa, *Zaïre* 28 E3
Kintyre, *U.K.* 10 F3
Kirghizia, ■ *Asia* 18 E8
Kiribati, ■ *Pac. Ocean* 3 D18
Kirkūk, *Iraq* 25 B3
Kirkcaldy, *U.K.* 10 E5
Kirkwall, *U.K.* 10 C6
Kiruna, *Swed.* 6 C15
Kisangani, *Zaïre* 28 D5
Kishinev, *Moldavia* 18 E3
Kitakyūshū, *Japan* 21 C2
Kitchener, *Canada* 35 D11
Kithira, *Greece* 15 F10
Kiva, L., *Africa* 28 E5
Kiyev, *Ukraine* 18 D4
Klagenfurt, *Austria* 16 E7
Knockmealdown Mts., *Ire.* 11 D4
Knossos, *Greece* 15 G11
Knoxville, *U.S.A.* 37 C10
Kobe, *Japan* 21 B4
København, *Den.* 7 J12
Koblenz, *Ger.* 16 C3
Kōchi, *Japan* 21 C3
Kodiak I., *Alaska* 34 C4
Kolding, *Den.* 7 J10
Köln, *Ger.* 16 C3
Komsomolsk, *Russia* 19 D14
Kongsvinger, *Norw.* 7 F11
Konya, *Turkey* 25 B2
Kopervik, *Norw.* 7 G8
Kopparberg, □ *Swed.* 7 F12
Kōriyama, *Japan* 21 G11
Kos, *Greece* 15 F12
Koŝice, *Slovak Rep.* 17 D10
Kosciusko, Mt., *Australia* 33 F8
Kosovo, □ *Yug.* 15 C9
Kowloon, *Hong Kong* 22 D6
Kraków, *Poland* 17 C9
Krasnodar, *Russia* 18 E4
Krasnoyarsk, *Russia* 19 D10
Krefeld, *Ger.* 16 C3
Kristiansand, *Norw.* 7 G10
Kristianstad, □ *Swed.* 7 J13
Kristiansund, *Norw.* 6 E9
Kriti, *Greece* 15 G11
Krivoy Rog, *Ukraine* 18 E4
Kronoberg, □ *Swed.* 7 H13
Kuala Lumpur, *Malaysia* 23 C2
Kumamoto, *Japan* 21 C2
Kumasi, *Ghana* 26 G4
Kuopio, □ *Fin.* 6 E19
Kure, *Japan* 21 B3
Kurashiki, *Japan* 21 B3
Kurilskiye Ostrova, *Russia* 19 E16
Kushiro, *Japan* 21 F11
Kuwait, ■ *Asia* 25 C3
Kuybyshev = Samara, *Russia* 18 D6
Kwangju, *S. Korea* 22 C7
Kyūshū, *Japan* 21 C2
Kyle of Lochalsh, *U.K.* 10 D3
Kyoga, L., *Uganda* 28 D6
Kyōto, *Japan* 21 B4
Kyiv = Kiyev, *Ukraine* 18 D4

L

La Boca, *Panama* 38 H14
La Chorrera, *Panama* 38 H14
La Coruña, *Spain* 13 A1
La Habana, *Cuba* 39 C8
La Paz, *Bolivia* 40 G5
La Plata, *Argentina* 42 D5
La Rioja, □ *Spain* 13 A4
La Rochelle, *France* 12 C3

Index

La Spézia, *Italy* 14 B3
Labrador, Coast of, *Canada* ...35 C13
Ladozhskoye, Ozero, *Russia* ...18 C4
Lagos, *Port.* 13 D1
Lagos, *Nigeria* 26 G5
Lahore, *Pak.* 24 B3
Lahti, *Fin.* 7 F18
Lakshadweep Is., *India* ...24 F3
Lancashire, □ *U.K.* 8 D5
Lancaster, *U.K.* 8 C5
Lancaster Sd., *Canada* ...35 A11
Landskrona, *Swed.* 7 J12
Languedoc, □ *France* ...12 E5
Lansing, *U.S.A.* 37 B10
Lanzhou, *China* 22 C5
Laois, □ *Ire.* 11 D4
Laos, ■ *Asia* 23 B2
Lapi, □ *Fin.* 6 C19
Lappland, *Fin.* 6 B18
Laptev Sea, *Arctic* 19 B13
Laredo, *U.S.A.* 36 E7
Lárisa, *Greece* 15 E10
Larne, *U.K.* 11 B6
Las Palmas, *Canary Is.* ...26 C1
Las Vegas, *U.S.A.* 36 C3
Latvia, ■ *Europe* 18 D3
Lauchhammer, *Ger.* 16 C6
Launceston, *Australia* ...33 G8
Lausanne, *Switz.* 16 E3
Lawton, *U.S.A.* 36 D7
Le Havre, *France* 12 B4
Le Mans, *France* 12 B4
Le Moule, *Guadeloupe* ...38 L20
Leamington, *U.K.* 9 E6
Lebanon, ■ *Asia* 25 B2
Lecce, *Italy* 15 D8
Leeds, *U.K.* 8 D6
Leeuwarden, *Neth.* 16 B2
Leeward Is., *W. Indies* ...39 D12
Legnica, *Poland* 16 C8
Leicester, *U.K.* 9 E6
Leicestershire, □ *U.K.* ...9 E6
Leiden, *Neth.* 16 B2
Leinster, □ *Ire.* 11 C4
Leipzig, *Ger.* 16 C6
Leith, *U.K.* 10 F5
Leitrim, □ *Ire.* 11 B3
Lena, ≈ *Russia* 19 B13
Leningrad = St. Peterburg, *Russia* ...18 D4
León, *Mexico* 38 C4
León, *Spain* 13 A3
Lérida, *Spain* 13 B6
Lesotho, ■ *Africa* 29 K5
Lesser Antilles, *W. Indies* ...39 E12
Lésvos, *Greece* 15 E11
Letchworth, *U.K.* 9 F7
Lethbridge, *Canada* ...34 D8
Leuven, *Belgium* 16 C2
Levkás, *Greece* 15 E9
Levkôsia, *Cyprus* 25 B2
Lewis, *U.K.* 10 C2
Lhasa, *China* 22 D4
Lianyungang, *China* ...22 C6
Liberec, *Czech. Rep.* ...16 C7
Liberia, ■ *Africa* 26 G3
Lîbïya, Sahrâ', *Africa* ...27 C9
Libreville, *Gabon* 28 D1
Libya, ■ *Africa* 27 C8
Liechtenstein, ■ *Europe* ...16 E4
Liège, *Belgium* 16 C2
Liffey, ≈ *Ire.* 11 C5
Liguria, □ *Italy* 14 B3
Ligurian Sea, *Italy* 14 C3
Likasi, *Zaïre* 28 G5
Lille, *France* 12 A5
Lillehammer, *Norw.* ...7 F11
Lilongwe, *Malawi* 29 G6
Lima, *Peru* 40 F3
Limavady, *U.K.* 11 A5
Limerick, *Ire.* 11 D3
Límnos, *Greece* 15 E11
Limoges, *France* 12 D4
Limousin, □ *France* ...12 D4
Limpopo, ≈ *Africa* 29 K6
Linares, *Spain* 13 C4
Lincoln, *U.S.A.* 37 B7
Lincoln, *U.K.* 8 D7
Lincolnshire, □ *U.K.* ...8 D7
Linköping, *Swed.* 7 G13
Linz, *Austria* 16 D7
Lisboa, *Port.* 13 C1
Lisburn, *U.K.* 11 B5
Listowel, *Ire.* 11 D2
Lithuania, ■ *Europe* 18 D3
Little Minch, *U.K.* 10 D2
Little Rock, *U.S.A.* 37 D8
Liverpool, *U.K.* 8 D5
Livingston, *U.K.* 10 F5
Livingstone, *Zambia* ...29 H5
Livorno, *Italy* 14 C4
Lizard, *U.K.* 11 H2
Ljubljana, *Slovenia* ...14 A6
Llanelli, *U.K.* 9 F3
Lloret, *Spain* 13 B7
Lobito, *Angola* 29 G2
Locarno, L. di, *Italy* ...14 A3
Lochaber, *U.K.* 10 E3
Lockerbie, *U.K.* 10 F5
Łódź, *Poland* 17 C9

Lofoten, *Norw.* 6 B12
Logroño, *Spain* 13 A4
Loire, ≈ *France* 12 C2
Lolland, *Den.* 7 J11
Lombardia, □ *Italy* 14 B3
Lombok, *Indonesia* 23 D3
Lomé, *Togo* 26 G5
Lomond, L., *U.K.* 10 E4
Lomza, *Poland* 17 B10
London, *U.K.* 9 F7
London, *Canada* 35 D11
Londonderry, *U.K.* 11 B4
Londrina, *Brazil* 42 A6
Long Beach, *U.S.A.* 36 D3
Long Island, *U.S.A.* ...37 B12
Longford, □ *Ire.* 11 C4
Lorca, *Spain* 13 D5
Lorne, *U.K.* 10 E3
Lorraine, □ *France* ...12 B7
Los Angeles, *U.S.A.* ...36 D3
Lothian, □ *U.K.* 10 F5
Loughborough, *U.K.* 8 E6
Louisiana, □ *U.S.A.* ...37 D8
Louisville, *U.S.A.* 37 C9
Lourdes, *France* 12 E3
Louth, □ *Ire.* 11 C5
Lower Hutt, *N.Z.* 31 J5
Lowestoft, *U.K.* 9 E9
Luanda, *Angola* 28 F2
Luanshya, *Zambia* ...29 G5
Lubbock, *U.S.A.* 36 D6
Lübeck, *Ger.* 16 B5
Lublin, *Poland* 17 C11
Lubumbashi, *Zaïre* 29 G5
Lucca, *Italy* 14 C4
Lucknow, *India* 24 C5
Ludwigshafen, *Ger.* 16 D4
Lugo, *Spain* 13 A2
Luleå, *Swed.* 6 D17
Lüneburger Heide, *Ger.* ...16 B5
Luoyang, *China* 22 C6
Lurgan, *U.K.* 11 B5
Lusaka, *Zambia* 29 H5
Luton, *U.K.* 9 F7
Luxembourg, ■ *Europe* ...16 D3
Luzern, *Switz.* 16 E4
Luzhou, *China* 22 D5
Luzon, *Philippines* 23 B4
Lvov, *Ukraine* 18 E3
Lycksele, *Swed.* 6 D15
Lymington, *U.K.* 9 G6
Lyon, *France* 12 D6

M

M'Clintock Chan., *Canada* ...34 B9
Macapá, *Brazil* 41 C8
Macau, ■ *Asia* 22 D6
Macclesfield, *U.K.* 8 D5
Macdonnell Ranges, *Australia* ...32 C5
Macedonia, ■ *Europe* 15 D9
Maceió, *Brazil* 41 E11
Mackenzie, ≈ *Canada* ...34 B6
Mackenzie Mts., *Canada* ...34 B6
Macroom, *Ire.* 11 E3
Madagascar, ■ *Africa* ...29 J9
Madeira, *Atl. Ocean* ...26 B1
Madeira, ≈ *S. Amer.* ...40 E6
Madhya Pradesh, □ *India* ...24 D4
Madras, *India* 24 F5
Madre, L., *Mexico* 38 B5
Madrid, □ *Spain* 13 B4
Madrid, *Spain* 13 B4
Madurai, *India* 24 G4
Maebashi, *Japan* 21 A6
Mafia I., *Tanzania* 28 F7
Magadan, *Russia* 19 D16
Magalluf, *Spain* 13 C7
Magdeburg, *Ger.* 16 B5
Magherafelt, □ *U.K.* ...11 B5
Maharashtra, □ *India* ...24 D4
Mahon, *Spain* 13 C8
Mai-Ndombe, L., *Zaïre* ...28 E3
Maidenhead, *U.K.* 9 F7
Maidstone, *U.K.* 9 F8
Maiduguri, *Nigeria* 27 F7
Maimana, *Afghan.* 25 B5
Maine, □ *France* 12 B3
Maine, □ *U.S.A.* 37 A13
Mainz, *Ger.* 16 D4
Makasar = Ujung Pandang, *Indonesia* 23 D3
Makedhona, □ *Greece* ...15 D10
Makgadikgadi Salt Pans, *Botswana* 29 J5
Makkah, *S. Arabia* 25 C3
Malaga, *Spain* 13 D3
Malatya, *Turkey* 25 B2
Malawi, ■ *Africa* 29 G6
Malaysia, ■ *Asia* 23 C2
Maldives, ■ *Ind. Ocean* ...24 G3
Mali, ■ *Africa* 26 E4
Mallorca, *Spain* 13 C7
Mallow, *Ire.* 11 D3
Malmö, *Swed.* 7 J12
Malmöhus, □ *Swed.* ...7 J12
Malta, ■ *Europe* 14 G6
Malvern Hills, *U.K.* 9 E5
Man, I. of, *U.K.* 8 C3

Managua, *Nicaragua* ...38 E7
Manaus, *Brazil* 40 D6
Manchester, *U.K.* 8 D5
Mandalay, *Burma* 24 D8
Mandla, L., *Canada* ...34 C10
Manila, *Philippines* ...23 B4
Manitoba, □ *Canada* ...34 C10
Manitoba, L., *Canada* ...34 C10
Manizales, *Colombia* ...40 B3
Mannheim, *Ger.* 16 D4
Monaghan, □ *Ire.* 11 B5
Mansel I., *Canada* ...35 B11
Mansfield, *U.K.* 8 D6
Mantova, *Italy* 14 B4
Maputo, *Mozambique* ...29 K6
Mar del Plata, *Argentina* ...42 D5
Maracaibo, *Venezuela* ...40 A4
Maracay, *Venezuela* ...40 A5
Marajó, I. de, *Brazil* ...41 D9
Maranhão, □ *Brazil* ...41 E9
Marbella, *Spain* 13 D3
Marche, ≈ *France* 12 C4
Marche, □ *Italy* 14 C5
Margate, *U.K.* 9 F9
Mariana Is., *Pac. Ocean* ...3 D17
Maribor, *Slovenia* 14 A6
Marie-Galante, *W. Indies* ...38 M20
Marília, *Brazil* 41 H8
Maringá, *Brazil* 42 A6
Marmara, Sea of, *Turkey* ...25 A1
Marquesas Is., *Pac. Ocean* ...2 J17
Marrakech, *Morocco* ...26 B3
Marseille, *France* 12 E6
Marshall Is., ■ *Pac. Ocean* ...3 D18
Martha's Vineyard, *U.S.A.* ...37 B12
Martinique, □ *W. Indies* ...38 N21
Maryland, □ *U.S.A.* ...37 C11
Mashhad, *Iran* 25 B4
Masqat, *Oman* 25 C4
Massachusetts, □ *U.S.A.* ...37 B12
Massif Central, *France* ...12 D5
Matadi, *Zaïre* 28 F2
Matamoros, *Mexico* 38 B5
Mato Grosso, □ *Brazil* ...41 F7
Mato Grosso do Sul, □ *Brazil* ...41 G7
Matsuyama, *Japan* 21 C3
Matterhorn, *Switz.* 16 E3
Maturín, *Venezuela* ...40 B6
Mauritania, ■ *Africa* ...26 E2
Mauritius, ■ *Ind. Ocean* ...30 H9
Mayo, □ *Ire.* 11 C2
Mazar-i-Sharif, *Afghan.* ...25 B5
Mbandaka, *Zaïre* 28 D3
Meath, □ *Ire.* 11 C5
Mecca = Makkah, *S. Arabia* ...25 C2
Mechelen, *Belgium* 16 C2
Medan, *Indonesia* 23 C1
Medellin, *Colombia* ...40 B3
Medicine Hat, *Canada* ...34 D8
Medina = Al Madinah, *S. Arabia* ...25 C2
Meerut, *India* 24 C4
Meknès, *Morocco* 26 B3
Mekong, ≈ *Asia* 23 B2
Melbourne, *Australia* ...33 F8
Melrose, *U.K.* 10 F6
Melville Is., *Australia* ...32 A5
Memphis, *U.S.A.* 37 C9
Menai Strait, *U.K.* 8 D3
Mendip Hills, *U.K.* 9 F5
Mendoza, *Argentina* ...42 C3
Menorca, *Spain* 13 B7
Mentawai Is., *Indonesia* ...23 D1
Merca, *Somalia* 30 F8
Mérida, *Mexico* 38 C7
Mersey, ≈ *U.K.* 8 D5
Merseyside, □ *U.K.* 8 D5
Merthyr Tydfil, *U.K.* 9 F4
Messina, *Italy* 14 E6
Metz, *France* 12 B7
Mexicali, *Mexico* 38 A1
Mexico, ■ *Cent. Amer.* ...38 D5
Mexico City, *Mexico* ...38 D5
Mexico, G. de, *Cent. Amer.* ...38 B6
Miami, *U.S.A.* 37 E10
Michigan, □ *U.S.A.* 37 A9
Michigan, L., *U.S.A.* ...37 B9
Micronesia, ■ *Pac. Ocean* ...3 D17
Mid Glamorgan, □ *U.K.* ...9 F4
Middlesbrough, *U.K.* 8 C6
Midland, *U.S.A.* 36 D6
Midland, *U.S.A.* 36 D6
Mikkeli, □ *Fin.* 6 E19
Milano, *Italy* 14 B3
Milton Keynes, *U.K.* 9 E7
Milwaukee, *U.S.A.* 37 B9
Minas Gerais, □ *Brazil* ...41 G9
Mindanao, *Philippines* ...23 C4
Minneapolis, *U.S.A.* 37 B8
Minnesota, □ *U.S.A.* ...37 A8
Minsk, *Belorussia* 18 D3
Miskolc, *Hungary* 17 D10
Misrâtah, *Libya* 27 B8
Mississippi, □ *U.S.A.* ...37 D9
Mississippi, ≈ *U.S.A.* ...37 E9
Missouri, □ *U.S.A.* 37 C8
Missouri, ≈ *U.S.A.* 37 C8
Miyako, *Japan* 21 G11
Miyazaki, *Japan* 21 D9
Mizoram, □ *India* 24 D9
Mobutu, L., *Africa* 28 D6
Moçambique, *Mozambique* ...29 H8
Módena, *Italy* 14 B4

Mogadishu, *Somalia* ...30 E8
Moldavia, ■ *Europe* ...18 E3
Molise, □ *Italy* 14 D6
Mölndal, *Swed.* 7 H12
Moluccas, *Indonesia* ...23 D4
Mombasa, *Kenya* 28 E7
Mona, Canal de la, *W. Indies* ...39 D11
Monaco, ■ *Europe* 12 E7
Monaghan, *Ire.* 11 B5
Mönchengladbach, *Ger.* ...16 C3
Moncton, *Canada* 35 D13
Mongolia, ■ *Asia* 22 B5
Monrovia, *Liberia* 26 G2
Mont St. - Michel, *France* ...12 B3
Montana, □ *U.S.A.* 36 A4
Monte Carlo, *Monaco* ...12 E7
Montes Claros, *Brazil* ...41 G10
Montenegro, □ *Yug.* 15 C8
Montevideo, *Uruguay* ...42 C5
Montgomery, *U.S.A.* 37 D9
Montpellier, *France* 12 E5
Montréal, *Canada* ...35 D12
Montrose, *U.K.* 10 E6
Montserrat, *W. Indies* ...38 L19
Moray Firth, *U.K.* 10 D5
More og Romsdal, □ *Norw.* ...6 E9
Morecambe B., *U.K.* 8 C4
Morelia, *Mexico* 38 D4
Morena, Sierra, *Spain* ...13 C3
Morioka, *Japan* 21 G11
Morocco, ■ *Africa* 26 B3
Morvern, *U.K.* 10 E3
Moscow = Moskva, *Russia* ...18 D4
Mosel, ≈ *Ger.* 16 C3
Moskva, *Russia* 18 D4
Mostaganem, *Algeria* ...26 A5
Motala, *Swed.* 7 G13
Motherwell, *U.K.* 10 F5
Moulamyaing, *Burma* ...24 E8
Mourne Mts., *U.K.* 11 B5
Mozambique, ■ *Africa* ...29 J6
Mozambique Chan., *Africa* ...29 H8
Muck, *U.K.* 10 E2
Mufulira, *Zambia* 29 G5
Mulhouse, *France* 12 C7
Mull, *U.K.* 10 E3
Mullet Pen., *Ire.* 11 B1
Mullingar, *Ire.* 11 C4
Multan, *Pak.* 24 B3
München, *Ger.* 16 D5
Munich = München, *Ger.* ...16 D5
Munster, *Ire.* 11 D3
Münster, *Ger.* 16 C3
Murcia, □ *Spain* 13 C5
Murmansk, *Russia* ...18 C4
Muroran, *Japan* 21 F11
Murray River, ≈ *Australia* ...33 F6
Murray River Basin, *Australia* ...33 E7
Musgrave Ranges, *Australia* ...32 D5
Mustique, *W. Indies* ...38 Q20
Mwanza, *Tanzania* 28 E6
Myanmar = Burma, ■ *Asia* ...24 D8
Mysore, *India* 24 F4

N

Nagano, *Japan* 21 A6
Nagaoka, *Japan* 21 G10
Nagasaki, *Japan* 21 C1
Nagoya, *Japan* 21 B5
Nagpur, *India* 24 D4
Nairobi, *Kenya* 28 E7
Nakhodka, *Russia* 19 E14
Namaland, *Namibia* ...29 J3
Namibia, ■ *Africa* 29 J3
Namibwoestyn, *Namibia* ...29 J2
Namsos, *Norw.* 6 D11
Namur, *France* 12 C6
Nanaimo, *China* 22 D6
Nanchang, *China* 22 D6
Nanjing, *China* 22 C6
Nanning, *China* 22 D5
Nansei-Shoto, *Japan* ...21 J8
Nantes, *France* 12 C3
Napier, *N.Z.* 31 H6
Napoli, *Italy* 14 D6
Narbonne, *France* 12 E5
Narvik, *Norw.* 6 B14
Naser, Buheiret en, *Egypt* ...27 D11
Nashville, *U.S.A.* 37 C9
Nassau, *Bahamas* 39 B9
Natal, *S. Africa* 29 K6
Natal, *Brazil* 41 E11
Nauru, ■ *Pac. Ocean* ...3 E18
Navarra, □ *Spain* 13 A5
Náxos, *Greece* 15 F11
Ndjamena, *Chad* 27 F8
Ndola, *Zambia* 29 G5
Nebraska, □ *U.S.A.* ...36 B6
Negro, ≈ *Brazil* 40 D6
Neiva, *Colombia* 40 C3
Nemuro, *Japan* 21 F12
Nemuro-Kaikyō, *Japan* ...21 F12
Nenagh, *Ire.* 11 D3
Nepal, ■ *Asia* 24 C5
Ness, L., *U.K.* 10 D4

Netherlands, ■ *Europe* ...16
Nevada, □ *U.S.A.* 36
Nevers, *France* 12
New Bedford, *U.S.A.* ...37
New Britain, *Pac. Ocean* ...3
New Brunswick, □ *Canada* ...35
New Caledonia, *Pac. Ocean* ...3
New Forest, *U.K.* 9
New Hampshire, □ *U.S.A.* ...37
New Haven, *U.S.A.* 37
New Jersey, □ *U.S.A.* ...37
New Mexico, □ *U.S.A.* ...36
New Orleans, *U.S.A.* ...37
New Plymouth, *N.Z.* 31
New Providence I., *W. Indies* ...39
New South Wales, □ *Australia* ...33
New York, *U.S.A.* 37
New York, □ *U.S.A.* 37
New Zealand, ■ *Pac. Ocean* ...31
Newark, *U.S.A.* 37
Newbury, *U.K.* 9
Newcastle, *Australia* 33
Newcastle-under-Lyme, *U.K.* ...8
Newfoundland, □ *Canada* ...35
Newport News, *U.S.A.* ...37
Newquay, *U.K.* 9
Newry, *U.K.* 11
Newtownabbey, □ *U.K.* ...11
Newtownards, *U.K.* 11
Niagara Falls, *N. Amer.* ...35
Niamey, *Niger* 26
Nicaragua, ■ *Cent. Amer.* ...38
Nice, *France* 12
Nicobar Is., *India* 24
Niederösterreich, □ *Austria* ...16
Niedersachsen, □ *Ger.* ...16
Niger, ■ *Africa* 26
Niger, ≈ *Africa* 26
Nigeria, ■ *Africa* 26
Nijmegen, *Neth.* 16
Nîl el Abyad, ≈ *Africa* ...27
Nîl el Azraq, ≈ *Africa* ...27
Nîl, Nahr en, ≈ *Africa* ...27
Nile = Nîl, Nahr en, ≈ *Africa* ...27
Nîmes, *France* 12
Ningbo, *China* 22
Nishinomiya, *Japan* ...21
Niteroi, *Brazil* 41
Nizhniy Novgorod, *Russia* ...18
Nord-Trondelag, □ *Norw.* ...6
Nordland, □ *Norw.* 6
Nordrhein - Westfalen, □ *Ger.* ...16
Norfolk, □ *U.S.A.* 37
Norfolk, □ *U.K.* 8
Normandie, □ *France* ...12
Norrbotten, □ *Norw.* 6
Norrköping, *Swed.* 7
North Carolina, □ *U.S.A.* ...37
North Channel, *Europe* ...8
North Dakota, □ *U.S.A.* ...36
North Downs, *U.K.* 9
North Island, *N.Z.* 31
North Korea, ■ *Asia* 22
North Minch, *U.K.* 10
North Ronaldsay, *U.K.* 10
North Sea, *Europe* 10
North Uist, *U.K.* 10
North West Highlands, *U.K.* ...10
North West Territories, □ *Canada* ...34
North Yorkshire, □ *U.K.* ...8
North Yorkshire Moors, *U.K.* ...8
Northampton, *U.K.* 9
Northamptonshire, □ *U.K.* ...9
Northern Ireland, □ *U.K.* ...11
Northern Territory, □ *Australia* ...32
Northumberland, □ *U.K.* ...8
Norway, ■ *Europe* 6
Norwegian Sea, *Atl. Ocean* ...6
Norwich, *U.K.* 8
Nottingham, *U.K.* 8
Nottinghamshire, □ *U.K.* ...8
Nouakchott, *Mauritania* ...26
Nova Scotia, □ *Canada* ...35
Novaya Zemlya, *Russia* ...18
Novi Sad, *Yug.* 15
Novokuznetsk, *Russia* ...18
Novosibirsk, *Russia* ...18
Novosibirskiye Ostrova, *Russia* ...19
Nûbïya, Es Sahrâ en, *Sudan* ...27
Nullarbor Plain, *Australia* ...32
Nuneaton, *U.K.* 9
Nunivak I., *Alaska* 34
Nürnberg, *Ger.* 16
Nyasa, L., *Africa* 29
Nykøbing, *Den.* 7

O

Oakland, *U.S.A.* 36
Ob, ≈ *Russia* 18
Oberhausen, *Ger.* 16
Oberösterreich, □ *Austria* ...16
Obihiro, *Japan* 21
Odense, *Den.* 7
Oder, ≈ *Europe* 16

ssa, Ukraine ...18 E4
ssa, U.S.A. ...36 D6
y, □ Ire. ...11 C4
nbach, Ger. ...16 C4
omosho, Nigeria ...26 G5
en, U.S.A. ...36 B4
, ≈ U.S.A. ...37 C9
, □ U.S.A. ...37 B10
vango Swamps, Botswana ...29 H4
yama, Japan ...21 B3
zaki, Japan ...21 B5
otsk, Russia ...19 D15
otsk Sea of, Arctic ...19 D15
Shotō, Japan ...21 A3
homa, □ U.S.A. ...37 C7
homa City, U.S.A. ...37 C7
shiri-Tō, Japan ...21 F10
d, Swed. ...7 H14
nburg, Ger. ...16 B4
am, U.K. ...8 D5
bos, Greece ...15 D10
nouc, Czech Rep. ...16 D8
npia, Greece ...15 F9
agh, U.K. ...11 B4
ha, U.S.A. ...37 B7
an, ■ Asia ...25 C4
an, Gulf of, Asia ...25 C4
lurmân, Sudan ...27 E11
a, Russia ...18 D8
ta, Japan ...21 C2
zhskoye, Ozero, Russia ...18 C4
sha, Nigeria ...26 G6
ario, □ Canada ...35 C11
ario, L., N. Amer. ...35 D12
va, Czech Rep. ...17 D8
land, □ Norw. ...7 F10
dea, Rom. ...17 E10
, Algeria ...26 A4
je, ≈ S. Africa ...29 K3
je-Vrystaat, □ S. Africa ...29 K5
oro, □ Swed. ...7 G13
gon, □ U.S.A. ...36 B2
nse, Spain ...13 A2
oco, ≈ S. Amer. ...40 B6
sa, □ India ...24 D5
hey, □ U.K. ...10 B5
ndo, U.S.A. ...37 E10
anais, □ France ...12 C4
ans, France ...12 C4
miyeh, Iran ...25 B3
o, Bolivia ...40 G5
ka, Japan ...21 B4
awa, Canada ...35 D12
ogbo, Nigeria ...26 G5
ek, Croatia ...15 B8
arshamn, Swed. ...7 H14
, Norw. ...7 G11
abrück, Ger. ...16 B4
rsund, Swed. ...6 E13
riesische Inseln, Ger. ...16 B3
ava, Czech Rep. ...17 D9
ov Vrangelya, Russia ...19 B18
mi-Kaikyō, Japan ...21 D2
mi-Shotō, Japan ...21 D2
u, Japan ...21 F11
nto, Str. of, Italy ...15 D8
wa, Canada ...35 D12
al, Austria ...16 E5
gadougou, Burkina Faso ...26 F4
da, Morocco ...26 B4
, Fin. ...6 D18
er Hebrides, U.K. ...10 D1
edo, Spain ...13 A3
mbo, Namibia ...29 H3
Mts., Ire. ...11 B4
ord, U.K. ...9 F6
rdshire, □ U.K. ...9 F6

araima, Sierra, S. Amer. ...40 C6
fic Ocean ...2 D3
ang, Indonesia ...23 D2
, Italy ...14 B4
ley, U.K. ...10 F4
stan, India ...24 C2
wan, Philippines ...23 B3
mbang, Indonesia ...23 D2
ncia, Spain ...13 A3
rmo, Italy ...14 E5
, Spain ...13 C7
nerston North, N.Z. ...31 J5
nira, Colombia ...40 C3
plona, Spain ...13 A5
ama, □ Cent. Amer. ...39 F8
ama Canal, Panama ...38 H14
ama City, Panama ...39 H14
ama, G. de, Panama ...39 F9
ua New Guinea, ■ Pac. Ocean ...3 E17
, □ Brazil ...41 D8
guay, ■ S. Amer. ...42 A5
iba, □ Brazil ...41 E11
amaribo, Surinam ...41 B7
ana, ≈ S. Amer. ...42 C5
aná, Argentina ...42 C4
cis, Serra dos, Brazil ...40 F6
, France ...12 C4
na, Italy ...14 B4

Pasadena, U.S.A. ...36 D3
Pasto, Colombia ...40 C3
Patna, India ...24 C6
Patos L. dos, Brazil ...42 C6
Patrai, Greece ...15 E9
Pavia, Italy ...14 B3
Pecs, Hungary ...17 E9
Peking = Beijing, China ...22 C6
Pelopónnisos, □ Greece ...15 F10
Pelotas, Brazil ...42 C6
Pemba I., Tanzania ...28 F7
Pennine Range, U.K. ...8 C5
Pennsylvania, □ U.S.A. ...37 B11
Pentland Firth, U.K. ...10 C5
Penzance, U.K. ...9 G2
Peoria, U.S.A. ...37 B9
Pereira, Colombia ...40 C3
Perm, Russia ...18 D6
Pernambuco, □ Brazil ...41 E11
Perpignan, France ...12 E5
Perth, Australia ...32 E2
Perth, U.K. ...10 E5
Peru, ■ S. Amer. ...40 E3
Perúgia, Italy ...14 C5
Pésaro, Italy ...14 C5
Pescara, Italy ...14 C6
Peshawar, Pak. ...24 B3
Peterboro', Canada ...35 D12
Peterborough, U.K. ...9 E7
Peterhead, U.K. ...10 D7
Petropavlovsk-Kamchatskiy, Russia 19 D16
Petrópolis, Brazil ...41 H10
Pforzheim, Ger. ...16 D4
Phanh Bho Ho Chi Minh, Vietnam ...23 B2
Philadelphia, U.S.A. ...37 B12
Philippi, Greece ...15 D11
Philippines, ■ Asia ...23 B4
Phnom Penh, Cambodia ...23 B2
Phoenix, U.S.A. ...36 D4
Phoenix Is., Pac. Ocean ...2 E1
Piacenza, Italy ...14 B3
Piauí, □ Brazil ...41 E10
Picardie, □ France ...12 A5
Piemonte, □ Italy ...14 B2
Pietermaritzburg, S. Africa ...29 K6
Pindos Oros, Greece ...15 E9
Piotrków Trybunalsk, Poland ...17 C9
Piracicaba, Brazil ...41 H9
Piraievs, Greece ...15 F10
Pisa, Italy ...14 C4
Pistóia, Italy ...14 C4
Piteå, Swed. ...6 D16
Pittsburgh, U.S.A. ...37 B11
Plauen, Ger. ...16 C6
Pleven, Bulg. ...15 C11
Ploieşti, Rom. ...17 F13
Plovdiv, Bulg. ...15 C11
Plymouth, U.K. ...9 G3
Plzeň, Czech Rep. ...16 D6
Po, ≈ Italy ...14 B5
Podgorica, Yug. ...15 C8
Pointe Noire, Congo ...28 E2
Pointe-à-Pitre, Guadeloupe ...38 L20
Poitou, □ France ...12 C3
Poland, ■ Europe ...17 C9
Ponce, Puerto Rico ...39 D11
Pondicherry, India ...24 F4
Ponta Grossa, Brazil ...42 B6
Pontefract, U.K. ...8 D6
Pontevedra, Spain ...13 A1
Pontiac, U.S.A. ...37 B10
Pontypool, U.K. ...9 F4
Pontypridd, U.K. ...9 F4
Poole, U.K. ...9 G6
Poona = Pune, India ...24 E3
Poopó, L., Bolivia ...40 G5
Popocatepetl, Mexico ...38 D5
Pori, Fin. ...7 F16
Port au Prince, Haiti ...39 D10
Port Elizabeth, S. Africa ...29 L5
Port Glasgow, U.K. ...10 F4
Port Harcourt, Nigeria ...26 H6
Port Laoise, Ire. ...11 C4
Port of Spain, Trinidad ...38 S20
Port Said = Bûr Saïd, Egypt ...27 B11
Port Talbot, U.K. ...9 F4
Portland, U.S.A. ...36 A2
Porto, Port. ...13 B1
Pôrto Alegre, Brazil ...42 C6
Portree, U.K. ...10 D2
Portsmouth, U.K. ...9 G6
Portsmouth, U.S.A. ...37 C11
Portugal, ■ Europe ...13 C1
Potosí, Bolivia ...40 G5
Potsdam, Ger. ...16 B6
Powys, □ U.K. ...9 F4
Poznan, Poland ...17 B9
Prague = Praha, Czech Rep. ...16 C7
Praha, Czech Rep. ...16 C7
Prato, Italy ...14 C4
Preston, U.K. ...8 D5
Pretoria, S. Africa ...29 K5
Prince Albert, Canada ...34 C9
Prince Charles I., Canada ...35 B12
Prince Edward I., □ Canada ...35 D13
Prince of Wales I., Alaska ...34 C6
Prince of Wales I., Canada ...34 A10
Provence, □ France ...12 E6
Providence, U.S.A. ...37 B12

Puebla, Mexico ...38 D5
Pueblo, U.S.A. ...36 C6
Puerto Rico, ■ W. Indies ...39 D11
Puglia, □ Italy ...14 D7
Pula, Croatia ...14 B5
Pune, India ...24 E3
Punjab, □ India ...24 B4
Purbeck, I. of, U.K. ...9 G5
Pusan, S. Korea ...22 C7
Pyongyang, N. Korea ...22 C7
Pyrénées, France ...12 E4

Q

Qatar, ■ Asia ...25 C4
Qingdao, China ...22 C7
Qiqihar, China ...22 B7
Quantock Hills, U.K. ...9 F4
Quebec, □ Canada ...35 C13
Quebec, Canada ...35 D12
Queen Charlotte Is., Canada ...34 C6
Queen Maud Gulf, Canada ...34 B9
Queensland, □ Australia ...33 C7
Quezon City, Philippines ...23 B4
Quito, Ecuador, ...40 D3

R

Rabat, Morocco ...26 B3
Radom, Poland ...17 C10
Ragusa, Italy ...14 F6
Rajasthan, □ India ...24 C3
Ramsgate, U.K. ...9 F9
Randers, Den. ...7 H11
Rangoon, Burma ...24 E8
Rasht, Iran ...25 B3
Rathlin I., U.K. ...11 A5
Rauma, Fin. ...7 F16
Ravenna, Italy ...14 B5
Rawalpindi, Pak. ...24 B3
Reading, U.K. ...9 F7
Rebun-Tō, Japan ...21 E11
Recife, Brazil ...41 E12
Red River, ≈ U.S.A. ...37 D8
Red Sea, Asia ...25 C3
Redditch, U.K. ...9 E6
Regensburg, Ger. ...16 D6
Réggio di Calábria, Italy ...14 E6
Réggio nell'Emília, Italy ...14 B4
Regina, Canada ...34 C9
Reichenbach, Ger. ...16 C6
Reigate, U.K. ...9 F7
Reims, France ...12 B6
Reina Adelaida, Arch., Chile ...42 G2
Reindeer L., Canada ...34 C9
Remscheid, Ger. ...16 C3
Rennes, France ...12 B3
Reno, U.S.A. ...36 C3
Réunion, □ Ind. Ocean ...30 H9
Reykjavik, Iceland ...6 D3
Rhein, ≈ Europe ...16 C3
Rheinland Pfalz, □ Ger. ...16 D3
Rhine = Rhein, ≈ Ger. ...16 C3
Rhode Island, □ U.S.A. ...37 B12
Rhodes = Ródhos, Greece ...15 F13
Rhodopi Planina, Bulg. ...15 D11
Rhôn, Ger. ...16 C5
Rhondda, U.K. ...9 F4
Rhône, ≈ France ...12 D6
Rhum, U.K. ...10 E2
Ribeirão Prêto, Brazil ...41 H9
Richmond, U.K. ...9 F7
Richmond, U.S.A. ...37 C11
Riga, Latvia ...18 D3
Rijeka, Croatia ...14 B5
Rimini, Italy ...14 B5
Rio Branco, Brazil ...40 E5
Rio de Janeiro, Brazil ...41 H10
Rio Gallegos, Argentina ...42 G3
Rio Grande, Brazil ...42 C6
Rio Grande do Norte, □ Brazil ...41 E11
Rio Grande do Sul, □ Brazil ...42 B6
Rishiri-Tō, Japan ...21 E11
Riyadh = Ar Riyād, S. Arabia ...25 C3
Rochefort, France ...12 D3
Rochester, U.K. ...9 F8
Rochester, U.S.A. ...37 B11
Rocky Mts., N. Amer. ...36 A4
Ródhos, Greece ...15 F13
Rogaland, □ Norw. ...7 G9
Roma, Italy ...14 D5
Romania, ■ Europe ...17 F12
Rondônia, □ Brazil ...40 F6
Roraima, □ Brazil ...40 C6
Roodepoort-Maraisburg, S. Africa ...29 K5
Rosario, Argentina ...42 C4
Roscommon, □ Ire. ...11 C3
Roseau, Dominica ...38 M20
Roskilde, Den. ...7 J12
Rostock, Ger. ...16 A6
Rostov, Russia ...18 E4
Rotterdam, Neth. ...16 C2
Roubaix, Belgium ...12 C1
Rouen, France ...12 B4
Rousay, U.K. ...10 B5
Ruse, Bulg. ...15 C10
Russia, ■ Europe/Asia ...18 C7
Rwanda, ■ Africa ...28 E5

Ryde, U.K. ...9 G6

S

's-Gravenhage, Neth. ...16 B2
's-Hertogenbosch, Neth. ...16 C2
Saarbrucken, Ger. ...16 D3
Saarland, □ Ger. ...16 D3
Sabadell, Spain ...13 B6
Sabah, □ Malaysia ...23 C3
Sacramento, U.S.A. ...36 C2
Sado, Japan ...21 G10
Safi, Morocco ...26 B3
Saginaw, U.S.A. ...37 B10
Sahara, Africa ...26 D4
Saigon = Phanh Bho Ho Chi Minh, Vietnam ...23 B2
Saint John, Canada ...35 D13
Saintonge, □ France ...12 D3
Sakai, Japan ...21 B4
Sakata, Japan ...21 G10
Sakhalin, Russia ...19 D15
Salamanca, Spain ...13 B3
Salerno, Italy ...14 D6
Salford, U.K. ...8 D5
Salisbury, U.K. ...9 F6
Salt Lake City, U.S.A. ...36 B4
Salta, Argentina ...42 A3
Saltillo, Mexico ...38 B4
Salvador, Brazil ...41 F11
Salzburg, Austria ...16 E6
Salzgitter, Ger. ...16 B5
Samara, Russia ...18 D6
Samarkand, Uzbekistan ...18 F7
Samoan Is., Pac. Ocean ...31 A12
Sámos, Greece ...15 F12
Samothráki, Greece ...15 D11
San Angelo, U.S.A. ...36 D6
San Antonio, U.S.A. ...36 E7
San Cristóbal, Venezuela ...40 B4
San Diego, U.S.A. ...36 D3
San Fernando, Trinidad ...38 S20
San Francisco, U.S.A. ...36 C2
San Francisco de Macoris, Dom. Rep. ...39 D10
San Jose, U.S.A. ...36 C2
San Juan, Argentina ...42 C3
San Juan, Puerto Rico ...39 D11
San Luis Potosi, Mexico ...38 C4
San Marino, ■ Europe ...14 C5
San Miguel de Tucuman, Argentina 42 B3
San Salvador, El Salvador ...38 E7
San Sebastian, Spain ...13 A4
San'a, Yemen ...25 D3
Sancti Spiritus, Cuba ...39 C9
Sanday, U.K. ...10 B6
Santa Ana, U.S.A. ...36 D3
Santa Barbara, U.S.A. ...36 D3
Santa Catarina, □ Brazil ...42 B7
Santa Clara, Cuba ...39 C9
Santa Clara, U.S.A. ...36 C2
Santa Cruz, Bolivia ...40 G6
Santa Cruz, Canary Is. ...26 C1
Santa Fe, Argentina ...42 C4
Santa Marta, Colombia ...40 A4
Santander, Spain ...13 A4
Santarém, Brazil ...41 D8
Santarém, Port. ...13 C1
Santiago, Chile ...42 C2
Santiago, Dom. Rep. ...39 D10
Santiago, Spain ...13 A1
Santiago de Cuba, Cuba ...39 C9
Santo Domingo, Dom. Rep. ...39 D11
Santos, Brazil ...42 A7
São Francisco, ≈ Brazil ...41 F11
São Luís, Brazil ...41 D10
São Paulo, □ Brazil ...41 H9
São Paulo, Brazil ...42 A7
São Tomé & Principe, ■ Africa ...30 E4
Sapporo, Japan ...21 F11
Sarajevo, Bosnia ...15 C8
Saratov, Russia ...18 D5
Sarawak, □ Malaysia ...23 C3
Sardegna, □ Italy ...14 D3
Sardinia = Sardegna, □ Italy ...14 D3
Sark, Channel Is. ...12 B2
Sasebo, Japan ...21 C1
Saskatchewan, □ Canada ...34 C9
Saskatoon, Canada ...34 C9
Satu Mare, Rom. ...17 E11
Saudi Arabia, ■ Asia ...25 C3
Sault Ste. Marie, Canada ...35 D11
Savannah, U.S.A. ...37 D10
Savoie, □ France ...12 D7
Savona, Italy ...14 B3
Scapa Flow, U.K. ...10 C5
Scarborough, U.K. ...8 C7
Schleswig - Holstein, □ Ger. ...16 A4
Schwäbische Alb, Ger. ...16 D4
Schwarzwald, Ger. ...16 D4
Schwerin, Ger. ...16 B5
Scilly, Is. of, U.K. ...9 H1
Scotland, □ U.K. ...10 E4
Scunthorpe, U.K. ...8 D7
Seattle, U.S.A. ...36 A2
Segovia, Spain ...13 B3
Seine, ≈ France ...12 B4
Sekondi - Takoradi, Ghana ...26 H4
Selkirk, U.K. ...10 F6

Semarang, Indonesia ...23 D3
Sendai, Japan ...21 G11
Senegal, ■ Africa ...26 F2
Serbia, □ Yug. ...15 C9
Setonaikai, Japan ...21 C3
Setúbal, Port. ...13 C1
Sevastopol, Ukraine ...18 E4
Severn, ≈ U.K. ...9 F5
Severnaya Zemlya, Russia ...19 B10
Sevilla, Spain ...13 D3
Seychelles, ■ Ind. Ocean ...3 E12
Sfax, Tunisia ...27 B7
Shache, China ...22 C2
Shanghai, China ...22 C7
Shannon, ≈ Ire. ...11 D2
Shantou, China ...22 D6
Shapinsay, U.K. ...10 B6
Sheffield, U.K. ...8 D6
Shenyang, China ...22 B7
Sherwood Forest, U.K. ...8 D6
Shetland, □ U.K. ...10 A7
Shikoku, Japan ...21 C3
Shimonoseki, Japan ...21 C2
Shiráz, Iran ...25 C4
Shizuoka, Japan ...21 B6
Sholapur, India ...24 E4
Shreveport, U.S.A. ...37 D8
Shrewsbury, U.K. ...8 E5
Shropshire, □ U.K. ...9 E5
Siam = Thailand, ■ Asia ...23 B2
Sibiu, Rom. ...17 F12
Sichuan, □ China ...22 D5
Sicilia, □ Italy ...14 F5
Siena, Italy ...14 C4
Sierra Leone, ■ Africa ...26 G2
Sierra Nevada, U.S.A. ...36 C3
Silver City, Panama ...38 H14
Simpson Desert, Australia ...32 C6
Singapore, ■ Asia ...23 C2
Sioux City, U.S.A. ...37 B7
Sioux Falls, U.S.A. ...37 B7
Siracusa, Italy ...14 F6
Sitges, Spain ...13 B6
Sjælland, Den. ...7 J11
Skagerrak, Europe ...7 H10
Skien, Norw. ...7 G10
Skikda, Algeria ...26 A6
Skopje, Macedonia ...15 C9
Skye, I. of, U.K. ...10 D2
Slieve Aughty, Ire. ...11 C3
Slieve Bloom, Ire. ...11 C4
Slieve Mish, Ire. ...11 D2
Sligo, Ire. ...11 B3
Slough, U.K. ...9 F7
Slovak Rep., ■ Europe ...17 D9
Slovenia, ■ Europe ...14 B6
Snake, ≈ U.S.A. ...36 A3
Snowdon, U.K. ...8 D3
Society Is., Pac. Ocean ...2 E2
Socotra, Yemen ...25 D4
Söderhamn, Swed. ...7 F14
Sofiya, Bulg. ...15 C10
Sogn og Fjordane, □ Norw. ...7 F9
Solimoes, ≈ Brazil ...40 D5
Solomon Is., ■ Pac. Ocean ...3 E17
Solway Firth, U.K. ...8 C4
Somali Rep., ■ Africa ...30 E8
Somerset, □ U.K. ...9 F4
Somerset I., Canada ...34 A10
Sor-Trondelag, □ Norw. ...6 D12
Soria, Spain ...13 B4
Sorocaba, Brazil ...42 A7
Sosnowiec, Poland ...17 C9
Sôul, S. Korea ...22 C7
Sousse, Tunisia ...27 A7
South Africa, ■ Africa ...29 L3
South Australia, □ Australia ...32 C6
South Bend, U.S.A. ...37 B9
South Carolina, □ U.S.A. ...37 D10
South China Sea, Asia ...23 B3
South Dakota, □ U.S.A. ...36 B6
South Downs, U.K. ...9 G7
South Georgia, Atl. Ocean ...42 G9
South Glamorgan, □ U.K. ...9 F4
South Island, N.Z. ...31 K3
South Korea, ■ Asia ...22 C7
South Ronaldsay, U.K. ...10 C6
South Shields, U.K. ...8 C6
South Uist, U.K. ...10 D1
South Yorkshire, □ U.K. ...8 D6
Southampton, U.K. ...9 F6
Southampton I., Canada ...35 B11
Southend, U.K. ...9 F8
Southern Alps, N.Z. ...31 K3
Southern Ocean ...3 G12
Southern Uplands, U.K. ...10 F5
Southport, U.K. ...8 D4
Soutpansberge, S. Africa ...29 J5
Spain, ■ Europe ...13 B4
Spandau, Ger. ...16 B6
Spanish Town, Jamaica ...38 K17
Spencer Gulf, Australia ...32 E6
Sperrin Mts., U.K. ...11 B4
Spessart, Ger. ...16 D4
Split, Croatia ...14 C7
Spokane, U.S.A. ...36 A3
Sporádhes Voríai, Greece ...15 E11
Springfield, U.S.A. ...37 B12
Springs, S. Africa ...29 K5

Index

Sri Lanka, ■ Asia ...24 G5
Srinagar, India ...24 B3
St. Albans, U.K. ...9 F7
St. Andrews, U.K. ...10 E6
St. Austell, U.K. ...9 G3
St. Boniface, Canada ...34 D10
St. Christopher-Nevis = St. Kitts - Nevis, ■ W. Indies ...38 K19
St. Croix, W. Indies ...39 D12
St. Étienne, France ...12 D6
St. Gallen, Switz. ...16 E4
St. George's, Grenada ...38 Q20
St. George's Channel, Europe ...11 E5
St. Helena, Atl. Ocean ...30 G3
St. Helens, U.K. ...8 D5
St. John's, Antigua ...38 K20
St. John's, Canada ...35 D14
St. Kitts - Nevis, ■ W. Indies ...38 K19
St. Lawrence, ≈ Canada ...35 D14
St. Louis, U.S.A. ...37 C8
St. Lucia, ■ W. Indies ...38 P21
St. Maarten, □ W. Indies ...38 J18
St. Malo, France ...12 B2
St. Martin, □ W. Indies ...38 J18
St. Michael's Mt., U.K. ...9 G2
St. Nazaire, France ...12 C2
St. Paul, U.S.A. ...37 B8
St. Peterburg, Russia ...18 D4
St. Petersburg, U.S.A. ...37 E10
St. Pierre et Miquelon, □ N. Amer. ...35 D14
St. Thomas, W. Indies ...39 D12
St. - Denis, France ...12 B5
St. - Tropez, France ...12 E7
St. Vincent & the Grenadines, ■ W. Indies ...38 P20
Stafford, U.K. ...8 E5
Staffordshire, □ U.K. ...8 E5
Staines, U.K. ...9 F7
Stalingrad = Volgograd, Russia ...18 E5
Stanley, Falkland Is. ...42 G5
Stara Planina, Bulg. ...15 C11
Stavanger, Norw. ...7 G8
Steiermark, □ Austria ...16 E7
Sterea Ellas, □ Greece ...15 E9
Stewart I., N.Z. ...31 M1
Stirling, U.K. ...10 E5
Stockholm, Swed. ...7 G15
Stockport, U.K. ...8 D5
Stockton, U.K. ...8 C6
Stockton, U.S.A. ...36 C2
Stoke-on-Trent, U.K. ...8 D5
Stonehenge, U.K. ...9 F6
Stourbridge, U.K. ...9 E5
Strabane, U.K. ...11 B4
Stralsund, Ger. ...16 A6
Strasbourg, France ...12 B7
Stratford-on-Avon, U.K. ...9 E6
Strath Spey, U.K. ...10 D5
Strathclyde, □ U.K. ...10 F3
Stromeferry, U.K. ...10 D3
Stronsay, U.K. ...10 B6
Stuttgart, Ger. ...16 D4
Subotica, Yug. ...15 A8
Sucre, Bolivia ...40 G5
Sudan, ■ Africa ...27 E10
Sudbury, Canada ...35 D11
Suez Canal, Egypt ...25 B2
Suez = El Suweis, Egypt ...27 C11
Suffolk, □ U.K. ...9 E8
Sulawesi, Indonesia ...23 D4
Sumatera, Indonesia ...23 D2
Sumba, Indonesia ...23 D4
Sumbawa, Indonesia ...23 D3
Sunderland, U.K. ...8 C6
Sundsvall, Swed. ...6 E14
Superior, L., N. Amer. ...37 A9
Surabaja, Indonesia ...23 D3
Surat, India ...24 D3
Surinam, ■ S. Amer. ...41 C7
Surrey, □ U.K. ...9 F7
Sutton-in-Ashfield, U.K. ...8 D6
Suva, Fiji ...31 D8
Suzhou, China ...22 C7
Svendborg, Den. ...7 J11
Sverdlovsk = Yekaterinburg, Russia 18 D7
Swansea, U.K. ...9 F4
Swaziland, ■ Africa ...29 K6
Sweden, ■ Europe ...7 F13
Swindon, U.K. ...9 F6
Switzerland, ■ Europe ...16 E3
Sydney, Australia ...33 E9
Syracuse, U.S.A. ...37 B11
Syria, ■ Asia ...25 B2
Syrian Desert, Asia ...25 B2
Szczecin, Poland ...16 B7
Szeged, Hungary ...17 E10

T

Tabriz, Iran ...25 B3
Tacoma, U.S.A. ...36 A2
Taegu, S. Korea ...22 C7
Tahiti, Pac. Ocean ...2 E2
Taibei, Taiwan ...22 D7
Tainan, Taiwan ...22 D7
Taiwan, ■ Asia ...22 D7
Taiyuan, China ...22 C6
Taizhong, Taiwan ...22 D7
Tajikistan, ■ Asia ...18 F7

Takamatsu, Japan ...21 B4
Talcahuano, Chile ...42 D2
Tallinn, Estonia ...18 D3
Tamil Nadu, □ India ...24 F4
Tampa, U.S.A. ...37 E10
Tampere, Fin. ...7 F17
Tampico, Mexico ...38 C5
Tamworth, U.K. ...9 E6
Tane-ga-Shima, Japan ...21 D2
Tanga, Tanzania ...28 F7
Tanganyika, L., Africa ...28 F5
Tanger, Morocco ...26 A3
Tangshan, China ...22 C6
Tanimbar Is., Indonesia ...23 D5
Tanta, Egypt ...27 B11
Tanzania, ■ Africa ...28 F7
Tarābulus, Lebanon ...25 B2
Tarābulus, Libya ...27 B7
Taranto, Italy ...14 D7
Tarragona, Spain ...13 B6
Tarrasa, Spain ...13 B6
Tashkent, Uzbekistan ...18 E7
Tasman Sea, Pac. Ocean ...31 J2
Tasmania, Australia ...33 G8
Tauern, Austria ...16 E6
Taunton, U.K. ...9 F4
Taunus, Ger. ...16 C4
Tay, ≈ U.K. ...10 E5
Tayside, □ U.K. ...10 E5
Tbilisi, Georgia ...18 E5
Tchad, L., Chad ...27 F7
Teesside, U.K. ...8 C6
Tegucigalpa, Honduras ...38 E7
Tehrān, Iran ...25 B4
Tehuantepec, Istme de, Mexico ...38 D6
Tejo, ≈ Port. ...13 C1
Tel Aviv - Yafo, Israel ...25 B2
Telemark, □ Norw. ...7 G10
Telford, U.K. ...8 E5
Tenerife, Canary Is. ...26 C1
Tennessee, □ U.S.A. ...37 C9
Tennessee, ≈ U.S.A. ...37 C9
Teresina, Brazil ...41 E10
Terni, Italy ...14 C5
Teruel, Spain ...13 B5
Tetouan, Morocco ...26 A3
Teutoburger Wald, Ger. ...16 B4
Tevere, ≈ Italy ...14 C5
Texas, □ U.S.A. ...36 D6
Thailand, ■ Asia ...23 B2
Thames, ≈ U.K. ...9 F8
Thásos, Greece ...15 D11
The Hague = 's-Gravenhage, Neth. .16 B2
Thessalia, □ Greece ...15 E10
Thessaloníka, Greece ...15 D10
Thies, Senegal ...26 F1
Thráki, □ Greece ...15 D11
Thunder Bay, Canada ...35 D11
Thüringer Wald, Ger. ...16 C5
Thurles, Ire. ...11 D4
Thurso, U.K. ...10 C5
Tianjin, China ...22 C6
Tiber = Tevere, ≈ Italy ...14 C5
Tibesti, Chad ...27 D8
Tibet = Xizang, □ China ...22 C3
Tientsin = Tianjin, China ...22 C6
Tierra del Fuego, S. Amer. ...42 G3
Tigris, ≈ Iraq ...25 B3
Tijuana, Mexico ...38 A1
Tilburg, Neth. ...16 C2
Timaru, N.Z. ...31 L3
Timișoara, Rom. ...17 F10
Timor, Indonesia ...23 D4
Tínos, Greece ...15 F11
Tipperary, □ Ire. ...11 D4
Tipperary, Ire. ...11 D3
Tipton, U.K. ...9 E5
Tirana, Alb. ...15 D8
Tiree, U.K. ...10 E2
Tirol, □ Austria ...16 E5
Tiruchchirappalli, India ...24 F4
Titicaca, L., S. Amer. ...40 G5
Titograd = Podgorica, Yug. ...15 C8
Tizi-Ouzou, Algeria ...26 A5
Tobago, W. Indies ...39 E12
Togo, ■ Africa ...26 G5
Tokelau Is., Pac. Ocean ...2 E1
Tōkyō, Japan ...21 B6
Toledo, Spain ...13 C3
Toledo, U.S.A. ...37 B10
Toluca, Mexico ...38 D5
Tomsk, Russia ...18 D9
Tonga, ■ Pac. Ocean ...31 D11
Toowoomba, Australia ...33 D9
Topeka, U.S.A. ...37 C7
Torbay, U.K. ...9 G4
Torino, Italy ...14 B2
Toronto, Canada ...35 D12
Torquay, U.K. ...9 G4
Torremolinos, Spain ...13 D3
Torrens, L., Australia ...33 E6
Torreón, Mexico ...38 B4
Tortosa, Spain ...13 B6
Toruń, Poland ...17 B9
Toscana, □ Italy ...14 C4
Toulon, France ...12 E6
Toulouse, France ...12 E4
Touraine, □ France ...12 C4
Tourcoing, Belgium ...16 C1

Tours, France ...12 C4
Townsville, Australia ...33 B8
Toyama, Japan ...21 A5
Toyohashi, Japan ...21 B5
Toyonaka, Japan ...21 B4
Tralee, Ire. ...11 D2
Transilvania, Rom. ...17 E12
Transvaal, □ S. Africa ...29 K5
Trápani, Italy ...14 E5
Trelleborg, Swed. ...7 J12
Trentino Alto-Adige, □ Italy ...14 A4
Treviso, Italy ...14 B5
Trier, Ger. ...16 D3
Trieste, Italy ...14 B5
Trincomalee, Sri Lanka ...24 G5
Trinidad & Tobago, ■ W. Indies ...39 E12
Tripoli = Tarābulus, Libya ...27 B7
Tristan da Cunha, Atl. Ocean ...2 F9
Trois-Rivières, Canada ...35 D12
Trollhättan, Swed. ...7 G12
Troms, □ Norw. ...6 B15
Tromsø, Norw. ...6 B15
Trondheim, Norw. ...6 E11
Trossachs, U.K. ...10 E4
Trujillo, Peru ...40 E3
Tsugaru-Kaikyō, Japan ...21 F11
Tsushima, Japan ...21 H8
Tuamotu Arch., Pac. Ocean ...2 E3
Tubuai Is., Pac. Ocean ...2 F2
Tucson, U.S.A. ...36 D4
Tula, Russia ...18 D4
Tullamore, Ire. ...11 C4
Tulsa, U.S.A. ...37 C7
Tulua, Colombia ...40 C3
Tunis, Tunisia ...26 A6
Tunisia, ■ Africa ...26 A6
Turin = Torino, Italy ...14 B2
Turkana, L., Kenya ...28 D7
Turkey, ■ Asia ...25 B2
Turkmenistan, ■ Asia ...18 F6
Turku, Fin. ...7 F17
Turnu-Severin, Rom. ...17 F11
Turun ja Pori, □ Fin. ...7 F17
Tuvalu, ■ Pac. Ocean ...3 E18
Tver, Russia ...18 D4
Tyler, U.S.A. ...37 D7
Tyne & Wear, □ U.K. ...8 C6
Tynemouth, U.K. ...8 C6
Tyrrhenian Sea, Italy ...14 E5

U

Uberaba, Brazil ...41 G9
Uddevalla, Swed. ...7 G11
Udine, Italy ...14 A5
Ufa, Russia ...18 D6
Uganda, ■ Africa ...28 D6
Ujpest, Hungary ...17 E9
Ujung Pandang, Indonesia ...23 D3
Ukraine, ■ Europe ...18 E4
Ulaanbaatar, Mong. ...22 B5
Ulan Ude, Russia ...19 D11
Ullapool, U.K. ...10 D3
Ulm, Ger. ...16 D4
Ulster, □ U.K. ...11 B4
Umbria, □ Italy ...14 C5
Ungava Pen., Canada ...35 C12
United Arab Emirates, ■ Asia ...25 C4
United Kingdom, ■ Europe ...4 E5
United States of America, ■ N. Amer. ...36 C6
Unst, U.K. ...10 A8
Uppsala, Swed. ...7 G14
Urmia, L., Iran ...25 B3
Uruguay, ■ S. Amer. ...42 C5
Uruguay, ≈ S. Amer. ...42 C5
Urumqi, China ...22 B3
Usti nad Labem, Czech Rep. ...16 C7
Utah, □ U.S.A. ...36 C4
Utrecht, Neth. ...16 B2
Utsunomiya, Japan ...21 A6
Uttar Pradesh, □ India ...24 C5
Uudenmaa, □ Fin. ...7 F18
Uzbekistan, ■ Asia ...18 E7

V

Vaal, ≈ S. Africa ...29 K4
Vaasa, □ Fin. ...6 E17
Vadso, Norw. ...6 A20
Valence, France ...12 D6
Valencia, □ Spain ...13 C5
Valencia, Spain ...13 C5
Valencia, Venezuela ...40 A5
Valladolid, Spain ...13 B3
Valle d'Aosta, □ Italy ...14 B2
Valletta, Malta ...14 G6
Valparaíso, Chile ...42 C2
Vancouver, Canada ...34 D7
Vancouver I., Canada ...34 D7
Vanuatu, ■ Pac. Ocean ...3 E18
Varanasi, India ...24 C5
Värmland, □ Swed. ...7 G12
Varna, Bulg. ...15 C12
Västerås, Swed. ...7 G14
Vasterbotten, □ Norw. ...6 D14
Vasternorrland, □ Norw. ...6 E14
Västervik, Swed. ...7 H14
Västmanland, □ Swed. ...7 G14

Vatnajökull, Iceland ...6 D5
Veneto, □ Italy ...14 B4
Venézia, Italy ...14 B5
Venezuela, ■ S. Amer. ...40 B5
Veracruz, Mexico ...38 D5
Vereeniging, S. Africa ...29 K5
Vermont, □ U.S.A. ...37 B12
Verona, Italy ...14 B4
Versailles, France ...12 B5
Vest-Agder, □ Norw. ...7 G9
Vesterålen, Norw. ...6 B13
Vestfjorden, Norw. ...6 B13
Vesuvio, Italy ...14 D6
Viborg, Den. ...7 H10
Vichy, France ...12 C5
Victoria, Australia ...33 F7
Victoria, Canada ...34 D7
Victoria Falls, Zimbabwe ...29 H5
Victoria I., Canada ...34 A8
Victoria, L., Africa ...28 E6
Vienna = Wien, Austria ...16 D8
Vientos, Paso de los, W. Indies ...39 C10
Vietnam, ■ Asia ...23 B2
Vigo, Spain ...13 A1
Vilnius, Lithuania ...18 D3
Viña del Mar, Chile ...42 C2
Virgin Is., W. Indies ...39 D12
Virginia, □ U.S.A. ...37 C11
Visby, Swed. ...7 H15
Vitória, Brazil ...41 H10
Vitoria, Spain ...13 A4
Vladivostok, Russia ...19 E14
Vojvodina, □ Yug. ...15 B8
Volga, ≈ Russia ...18 E5
Volgograd, Russia ...18 E5
Vólos, Greece ...15 E10
Volta, L., Ghana ...26 G4
Vorarlberg, □ Austria ...16 E4
Voronezh, Russia ...18 D4
Vyatka, Russia ...18 D5

W

Waco, U.S.A. ...37 D7
Wâd Medanî, Sudan ...27 F11
Wakayama, Japan ...21 B4
Wakefield, U.K. ...8 D6
Wakkanai, Japan ...21 E11
Wałbrzych, Poland ...16 C8
Wales, □ U.K. ...9 E4
Wallasey, U.K. ...8 D4
Wallsend, U.K. ...8 B6
Walney I., U.K. ...8 C4
Walsall, U.K. ...9 E6
Walvisbaai, S. Africa ...29 J2
Wanganui, N.Z. ...31 H5
Warley, U.K. ...9 E6
Warrington, U.K. ...8 D5
Warszawa, Poland ...17 B10
Warwick, U.K. ...9 E6
Warwickshire, □ U.K. ...9 E6
Wash, The, ≈ U.K. ...8 E8
Washington, □ U.S.A. ...36 A2
Washington D.C., U.S.A. ...37 C11
Waterbury, U.S.A. ...37 B12
Waterford, Ire. ...11 D4
Watford, U.K. ...9 F7
Weald, The, U.K. ...9 F7
Welkom, S. Africa ...29 K5
Wellesley Is., Australia ...33 B6
Wellington, N.Z. ...31 J5
Wellington I., Chile ...42 F2
Wenzhou, China ...22 D7
West Bromwich, U.K. ...9 E6
West Glamorgan, □ U.K. ...9 F4
West Indies ...39 D10
West Midlands, □ U.K. ...9 E6
West Sussex, □ U.K. ...9 G7
West Virginia, □ U.S.A. ...37 C10
West Yorkshire, □ U.K. ...8 D6
Western Australia, □ Oceania ...32 C3
Western Is., □ U.K. ...10 D1
Western Sahara, ■ Africa ...26 C2
Western Samoa, ■ Pac. Ocean ...2 E1
Westerwald, Ger. ...16 C3
Westmeath, □ Ire. ...11 C4
Weston-super-Mare, U.K. ...9 F6
Westray, U.K. ...10 B5
Wexford, Ire. ...11 D5
Weymouth, U.K. ...9 G5
Whalsay, U.K. ...10 A8
White Nile = Nîl el Abyad, ≈ Africa ...27 E11
White Sea = Beloye More, Russia ...18 C4
Whitehaven, U.K. ...8 C4
Whitehorse, Canada ...34 B6
Wichita, U.S.A. ...37 C7
Wichita Falls, U.S.A. ...36 D7
Wick, U.K. ...10 C5
Wicklow, Ire. ...11 D5
Wien, Austria ...16 D8
Wiesbaden, Ger. ...16 C4
Wigan, U.K. ...8 D5
Wight, I. of, □ U.K. ...9 G6
Wilhelmshaven, Ger. ...16 B4
Wilmington, U.S.A. ...37 C11
Wiltshire, □ U.K. ...9 F6
Winchester, U.K. ...9 F6
Windermere, L., U.K. ...8 C5
Windhoek, Namibia ...29 J3

Windsor, U.K. ...9
Windsor, Canada ...35
Windward Is., W. Indies ...39
Winnipeg, Canada ...34
Winnipeg, L., Canada ...34
Winston Salem, U.S.A. ...37
Winterthur, Switz. ...16
Wirral, The, U.K. ...8
Wisconsin, □ U.S.A. ...37
Wishaw, U.K. ...10
Włocławek, Poland ...17
Woking, U.K. ...9
Wollongong, Australia ...33
Wolverhampton, U.K. ...9
Worcester, U.K. ...9
Worcester, U.S.A. ...37
Workington, U.K. ...8
Worksop, U.K. ...8
Worms, Ger. ...16
Worthing, U.K. ...9
Wrexham, U.K. ...8
Wrocław, Poland ...16
Wuhan, China ...22
Wuhu, China ...22
Wuppertal, Ger. ...16
Würzburg, Ger. ...16
Wyoming, □ U.S.A. ...36

X

Xi'an, China ...22
Xiaguan, China ...22
Xingu, ≈ Brazil ...41
Xinjiang Uygur, □ China ...22
Xizang, □ China ...22
Xuzhou, China ...22

Y

Yakushima, Japan ...21
Yakutsk, Russia ...19
Yamagata, Japan ...21
Yaoundé, Cameroon ...28
Yaroslavl, Russia ...18
Yazd, Iran ...25
Yell, U.K. ...10
Yellow Sea, Asia ...22
Yellowknife, Canada ...34
Yellowstone National Park, U.S.A. ..36
Yemen, ■ Asia ...25
Yenisey, ≈ Russia ...18
Yeovil, U.K. ...9
Yerevan, Armenia ...18
Yining, China ...22
Yokohama, Japan ...21
Yokosuka, Japan ...21
York, U.K. ...8
Youghal, Ire. ...11
Ystad, Swed. ...7
Yucatan, □ Mexico ...38
Yugoslavia, ■ Europe ...15
Yukon, ≈ N. Amer. ...34
Yukon Territory, □ Canada ...34

Z

Zabrze, Poland ...17
Zagazig, Egypt ...27
Zagreb, Croatia ...14
Zagros Mts., Iran ...25
Zaïre, ≈ Africa ...28
Zaïre, ■ Africa ...28
Zákinthos, Greece ...15
Zambezi, ≈ Africa ...29
Zambia, ■ Africa ...29
Zamora, Spain ...13
Zanzibar, Tanzania ...28
Zaporozhye, Ukraine ...18
Zaragoza, Spain ...13
Zaria, Nigeria ...26
Zemlya Frantsa Iosifa, Russia ...18
Zhanghua, Taiwan ...22
Zhangjiakou, China ...22
Zhengzhou, China ...22
Zhenjiang, China ...22
Zibo, China ...22
Zigong, China ...22
Zimbabwe, ■ Africa ...29
Zürich, Switz. ...16
Zwickau, Ger. ...16